Who Do
YOU Say
I AM ?

by

Ken Hubbard

Who Do You Say I Am?

Published by:

Serenity Books
P.O. Box 3595
Hagerstown, MD 21742-3595

ISBN 1-58158-062-2

Printed in the United States of America
For Worldwide Distribution

Dedication

I want to dedicate this book to the five original board members who brought me in at twenty-seven years old to candidate to a church that was hurting and starving for leadership. It took a great deal of courage and faith for these men to catch the vision and to put their trust in a young, inexperienced pastor with no Bible college background, but just a great vision to do a great work for the Kingdom. I want to thank you men for hearing the voice of God. It has been an incredible journey.

Dave Trent was the pulpit search chairman, and the others on that committee were Jerry Ryan, Bret Smith, Bob Wolf and Bill Burley. You men endured some rough and tough days at United, but thanks for sticking to it when times got tough. Today, what God is doing in our midst is truly a result of your tenacity, your strength, and your courage. You held onto the vision that one day God would bring a great move of the Spirit to United Assembly of God (R.O.C.), and we are all now seeing the fulfillment of your vision.

Contents

Introduction

In this book, you will read many testimonies of what God has done through the ministry efforts at United Assembly of God.

While the name of our church has changed (we are now Revival Outreach Center), we have chosen to leave the original name of the church in all of the testimonies because that was the name of the church during all of these particular life changes.

As I read through the wonderful testimonies of these precious people who tell their stories of who Jesus is to them, I continue to be blessed, and I am reminded of the amazing grace of God. Even since the publication of this book, many stories have had a "part two" that make the lives of these people even more exciting.

I find myself becoming very uncomfortable as I notice how often people thank God for using me. The words "Pastor Hubbard" show up way more often than I feel comfortable with. In the editing process of this book, I began going through the pages crossing my name out of each testimony. The Spirit of God spoke to me then and reminded me that God always chooses people to accomplish His great work. So, I leave my name in, not as one desiring or even comfortable with seeing my name so many times, but as an example to others of what God can do with a life that is submitted to Him.

Many of you who read this book may know me and my story personally. Jesus created who I am today from a kid who had absolutely no aspirations and no hopes of ever being anybody. He has turned my life around. What the devil meant for harm is now to the benefit of God's Kingdom.

When I look at all the testimonies of who these people say Jesus is, I begin to ponder who I say He is, and the best word I have is that Jesus is my everything! In fact, the very epitome of who I am is wrapped up in who He is.

His Word is true: He will truly be a Father to the fatherless. As a child, I was often discouraged without a father in my life. When going into the ministry, I was discouraged that I didn't have the right connections, the right friendships, the right mentorships, but the Lord has taught me that when He is all that you have, He is all that you need. He has been my Father, my Friend and my Mentor.

As you read through the pages of this book and as you read the wonderful testimonies of transformed lives, I want you to be reminded of the words Moses spoke in the book of Exodus when he asked, "Who shall I say sent me?" The Great Voice From Heaven answered him, "Tell them I AM THAT I AM."

The Lord's response is as if He said and is still saying, "I AM ... you fill in the blank," meaning He is whatever we need Him to be: Father, Friend, Comforter, Protector, Healer, Helper, Deliverer.... The list is endless. It is impossible to describe all that God is because He's so big, so great, so deep and so wide that if we were able to explain Him, we would become as gods ourselves. However, His ways are higher than our ways, so it is impossible for us to comprehend all that He is. Through our testimonies, we try to define Him, but He is bigger than any definition we could possibly offer.

Today, if you are longing and searching because you have

emptiness in your life and you have somehow picked up this book, know that you are not alone. Read the testimonies of the others in this book who have been where you are today. You can find your everything in Him too! By simply bowing your knee and admitting that you are a sinner, you can ask Jesus Christ to come into your life to be your Lord and Savior. Then the Great I AM THAT I AM will fill in your blanks, so that you too can experience His life-changing power!

Part One

Who Do They Say I AM?

When Jesus came to the region of Caesarea Philippi, he asked his disciples, "Who do people say the Son of Man is?"

They replied, "Some say John the Baptist; others say Elijah; and still others, Jeremiah or one of the prophets."

"But what about you" he asked. "Who do you say I am?"

Simon Peter answered, "You are the Christ, the Son of the living God."

Jesus replied, "Blessed are you, Simon son of Jonah, for this was not revealed to you by man, but by my Father in heaven. And I tell you that you are Peter, and on this rock I will build my church, and the gates of Hades will not overcome it. I will give you the keys of the kingdom of heaven; whatever you bind on earth will be bound in heaven, and whatever you loose on earth will be loosed in heaven."

Matthew 16:13-19

One evening my wife, Patti, turned on the TV, and we caught the last five minutes of a movie. Once before, we had caught the same last five minutes of the same movie.

"This is terrible!" Patti said. "We can never see this movie because we already know the ending." How boring is that?!

It is somewhat the same when we know the ending of a Bible story. We often race through it, reading it with less intensity, less passion, losing the human drama.

The text in Matthew sixteen is one that Christians have become so familiar with that the dynamics of it are often lost. We quite defensively quote the last part of verse nineteen: *"and the gates of Hades* [Hell] *will not overcome* [prevail against] *it,"* but I believe God desires us to view this passage of scripture *offensively* and to use it that way as well.

It's true that we can overcome what the devil shovels out, but why should we wait for the devil to "happen" to us? I believe God wants to raise up a generation that is going to "happen" to the devil!

How does this happen? Jesus gave the keys to binding and loosing things in Heaven and on Earth after Peter received the revelation of who Jesus is. The key to binding (prohibiting) the enemy and loosing (permitting) the Holy Spirit to do the Father's will is *getting a revelation of who Jesus is*. This revelation is powerful and will change your life!

If we asked people today who Jesus is, some might say He is a good man; some might say He is a prophet or a great teacher.

Tragically, we live at a time when people try to make Jesus what they want Him to be and seek Him only when they need Him.

When there is a crisis, they pull Him out; when there is peace, they put Him away. When planes fly into the World Trade Center, they pull Him out; when the fire is burned out, they put Him away.

When I can't pay the bills, I pull Him out; when I'm paying the bills, I put Him away. When I'm sick, I pull Him out; when I'm happy, I put Him away.

People come into our churches to find out who Jesus is, and what we proclaim about Him ultimately determines who they say He is. Unfortunately, we have not always rightly proclaimed who Jesus is, so they leave our churches to build their own gods.

Teenagers flock to a singer by the name of Marilyn Manson. He once sat on the front row of a church, trying to find the answer to "Who do you say Jesus is?" Woefully, the Church gave him a twisted, warped and mutated version of who Jesus is. This twisted image is getting passed on to a generation that is looking to follow someone.

Today's cult leaders and occult leaders take others down paths of destruction because they came into the Church asking, "Who do you say Jesus is?" seeking for the Church to supply the answer, but the Church stuttered.

The Church stuttered because there are too many people sitting in our pews who have only a secondhand revelation of who Jesus is. They have no personal, firsthand experience with His salvation, with His healing or with His glory.

In the scripture passage from Matthew, Peter was the only disciple out of the twelve to rise up and answer the Lord.

"You are the Christ, the Son of the living God."
Jesus replied, "Blessed are you, Simon son of Jonah,
for this was not revealed to you by man, but by my
Father in heaven."

Peter had a firsthand revelation of who Jesus was.

We each need a personal, firsthand revelation of what God reveals about Jesus, not a secondhand revelation. God Himself must reveal to us who Jesus is, not the pastor, your church or your parents. Having a personal revelation of Jesus means you've been around Him enough that *you* know Him.

You will find that He is so deep you can't get under Him, so high you can't get over Him, so wide you can't get around Him. And His mercies are new every day. A firsthand revelation comes because God is with you and He speaks to you.

Jesus said to Simon Peter, *"I tell you that you are Peter, and on this rock I will build my church."* A church centered on this statement is built on the revelation that He is the Son of the living God. This church is not built on fads; this church is not built on traditions; it is built on the fact that He is Christ, and not just the Christ we say He is, but also the Christ who is revealed in us who make up His Body.

I believe there are three types of churches being built in America today. One is the **"systematic church."** The systematic church is the church that has become very "religious," enslaved to tradition—having repetition without revelation.

The systematic church produces people with a survivalist mindset, who live in the land of "not enough." It is a tragic thing when, as a child of God with the wealth of Heaven, we live in the land of not enough: not enough joy, not enough peace, not enough hope, not enough God, not enough Holy Ghost.

The people in this church are hungry because they are

living with a survivalist mindset. They scrounge to find something to eat, but the only thing being served is left over from yesterday. So they rummage through the religion; they rummage through the systems; they rummage through the programs; they rummage through the rhetoric, trying to find some reality in the midst of the rhetoric. They have become starving people.

Such was the church at Corinth—without the Spirit of God and steeped in tradition.

> *The man without the Spirit does not accept the things that come from the Spirit of God, for they are foolishness to him, and he cannot understand them, because they are spiritually discerned.*
>
> First Corinthians 2:14

If this is the message the systematic church offers, if this is the Christ portrayed to the world, then it is no wonder that the world doesn't know who Jesus is when looking to a systematic church.

Another type of church in America today is the **"secular church."** They have a form of godliness but have no power. They are like the church in Galatians 1:6-7.

> *I am astonished that you are so quickly deserting the one who called you by the grace of Christ and are turning to a different gospel—which is really no gospel at all.*

What is this *"different gospel"*? It is a "secular" gospel that doesn't preach repentance; it is a gospel that wears a cross but doesn't bear a cross; it is a gospel that won't say one has to die to self. In secular churches, there is no singing about the blood of Jesus and there are no altar calls.

The secular church produces carnal, worldly saints because it doesn't teach repentance. There is no physical, outward demonstration of an inward change.

The secular church lives in the land of "just enough." These folks have "just enough" to look good in the world and look good in the church too. They have just enough to hang with the fellas and the deacons, and they have just enough to fit in at the club and at the church. They have just enough to look successful.

Secular churches can draw a crowd, but they can't build a congregation. People come because they are drawn to the polish of the program, but quickly find there is not as much substance in this church as they had needed or hoped for.

The secular church is filled with the immature in the faith because they can't grow up. Come Monday morning, you can't tell the secular believer from his unsaved neighbor.

The image of Christ the secular church presents to the world is hazy, wavering and incomplete. How can this message tell anyone who Jesus really is?

Today, Jesus is actively building the third type of church, the **"supernatural church,"** a led-by-the-Spirit church—the church He will bless! This church is no longer governed by politics, programs and polish.

Jesus said:

> *"And I tell you that you are Peter and on this rock I will build my church, and the gates of Hades will not overcome it. I will give you the keys of the kingdom of*

heaven; whatever you bind on earth will be bound in heaven, and whatever you loose on earth will be loosed in heaven."

Matthew 16:18-19

Jesus said this church possesses the keys to unlock the Kingdom of Heaven!

So, why are the things we want and need locked up? It is not because the devil (or Hell) has authority over them, but because we have not yet received, as Peter did, the powerful revelation of who God says Jesus is, and that is the *key* that unlocks the Kingdom.

Before, when I read Jesus' words about "Hell shall not prevail," I thought He meant the devil was the one always on the attack and we were always on the defensive, but that's just silly. The only reason he has *any* power is because we *give* him power.

When we get a revelation of who Jesus is, we will no longer let the devil push us around. We will have an understanding of who we are, because we understand who He is. It is this revelation that *turns* the keys to unlock the Kingdom!

In Bible times, the scribes used to wear a key sewn into the fabric of their shirt, or tunic, symbolizing that they had the key to unlock the blessing of the Scriptures.

That is what Jesus meant when He said, "Peter, I'm going to give you the keys because you have had a revelation. The gates *will not* prevail against you, because you see Me for who I really am. The gates of Hell cannot push you around."

We have the keys to unlock things from the past. We can unlock unsaved loved ones and bring them out, and the gates of Hell shall not prevail against us. We can unlock wealth, we can unlock health, and the gates of Hell shall not prevail against us.

But that's only part of His promise. He also said that whatever we loose on Earth will be loosed in Heaven, and whatever we bind on Earth will be bound in Heaven.

This is how we *use* the keys. I can hear the theological critic saying, "But what about the health you just released? I'm still sick." The truth is the gates of Hell won't prevail; you *will* get your healing.

Here is how I know: because He *is* the healing, and when you pray for God to heal you, He doesn't have to *find* the answer—He *is* the answer. And when you get the revelation that He is the answer—He is the health—you have the keys to open up (loose from Heaven) healing, and the gates of Hell will not prevail against you.

On Earth, we're confined to the moment. But Jesus said that whatever is loosed on Earth will be loosed in Heaven. It might show up on Earth, it might show up in Heaven, but it is loosed in all realms. And the gates of Hell shall not prevail against it.

When you begin to understand Jesus' question: "Who do you say I am?" and when you get a revelation of who He is—the Christ, the Alpha and Omega, the beginning and the end—you will jump up and say, as Peter did, "You are the Christ, the Son of the living God!"

As a corporate body, we represent the image of Jesus to the world, and the world decides who Jesus is based on who we say He is. After all, Jesus is the head of His Church, but the Church is the Body, and it's the Church that represents Jesus in the world. So the world not only looks to the Church to find out who we say Jesus is, but the world also looks to the Church to *be* who Jesus is. And if the Church has not healed anyone, how can the world believe Jesus heals? If the Church has not changed lives, how can the world believe Jesus changes lives?

To this point, we have talked in terms of various churches, but don't be deceived. As an individual believer, you can sit in a supernatural church and all the while be a "systematic" (religious) person with no power. You can be in the supernatural church, but be a secular "church" in yourself. My friend, this message is for *you*, personally. When your neighbor asks you who Jesus is and looks at your life, are your words and your life compatible with the answer? Is Jesus the Son of the living God in your church and in your life? Where is your evidence?

Jesus is asking you today, "Who do *you* say I AM?"

Part Two

Who Do You Say I AM?

The following testimonies are given by people who are a part of the Lord's Body at the United Assembly of God Church in Plymouth, Michigan. Through their stories of the Lord's provision, healing and deliverance, they have found the answer to who Jesus is, because they have seen and experienced Him working in their lives through His Church. These are people who now have a firsthand revelation of Jesus Christ and are prepared to share with the world their answers to Jesus's question: "Who do you say I AM?"

Tammy Allen: Jesus Is My Righteousness

That which Satan meant for evil God has turned to good. Our testimony is a perfect example of just that and a beautiful picture of God's heart concerning restoration in marriage.

I want to start by saying the Lord is so faithful, and apart from Him we are and have nothing! My husband, Tim, and I live that reality, but for us that reality came at a price. God allowed our marriage to seem hopeless.

In 1998 I had an affair with another man. It lasted for almost one year. Wow! Even now in writing this it seems so devastating, but the fact is, an affair doesn't "just happen" as we often hear people say. It starts with deception, which creeps in through the smallest things. Satan comes in very subtly—at least for me he did. I began to believe the lies of the enemy. I started feeling that my husband didn't love me.

Tim and I were never very good at communicating with each other, and intimacy was just out of the question. Satan saw what was happening in our marriage, and I realize now that he has a plan for our lives just as God does.

The other man began saying things to me to make me feel significant that my husband used to say. That was huge for me, so I became infatuated with him. We began to "hang out" after work and to have intimate conversations. Needless to say, before long it became physical. I was so deceived that after about six months I was ready to leave Tim and marry this other person. When I think of how close I came to losing my family, it still causes me to shudder.

I continued to go to church and fulfill what was expected of me at home. At this point Tim still didn't know about the affair. He knew I was falling away from the Lord, but he didn't know to what degree. When he realized I had started drinking heavily and hanging with the wrong people, he began to pray for me, fervently.

Tim had told me for years that if I ever cheated on him he would divorce me—no questions asked. But that was the last thing in the world he thought I would ever do, and so did I. We never dreamed this could happen to us. I've found the small things that can creep into your spirit when you don't guard your heart can and will eventually devastate your world.

Tim found out about the affair through a friend of his sister, Karen, whom I now realize was being obedient to the Lord by what she did (and I will always be grateful). When Tim confronted me with what he knew, I almost felt relieved because now I didn't have to lead two lives anymore and I could marry this other man. (How deceived was I? I cannot stress enough how critical it is to not let yourself be deceived by lies of the enemy—stay tuned in to God's voice!)

I will never forget the look of brokenness on Tim's face when he saw my response. I had never seen anyone so devastated. To think of it now breaks my heart, but at the time, I didn't care what he was feeling. I know I seemed like a cold-hearted jerk with no feelings, but I really felt justified. I had spent the first five years of our marriage as a submissive servant for my husband and my children.

But, at the same time, I realized just how much Tim did love me. From that moment on, Tim committed himself to prayer concerning our marriage. He and his family would meet once a week to pray for me. And from what I understand now, there were specific nights on which they prayed that God intervened in my life. I might not be here today if it weren't for their prayers.

Plymouth United, or I guess I should say the *people* of

Plymouth United, were so instrumental in my deliverance and in the healing and restoration of our marriage. We came to United about four years ago, and we started counseling with Pastor Whittum.

I want to say thank you to him and his wife, Cheryl. He is an awesome marriage counselor who truly hears from the Lord. And thank you, Cheryl, because without you he couldn't be who he is.

My deliverance came on a Sunday night. I slipped into service late (after being at a bar), thinking that I would simply make an appearance and go home. Tim was out of town, and I was supposed to be in church, so I came in and sat in the back so no one would talk to me and I could get out of there.

But God (my two favorite words) had other plans. A prayer partner came to me and said, "Can I pray for you?" Still feeling intoxicated from earlier that day, I said, "Sure!"

I got up and six or eight people started to pray for me. The next thing I knew I was on the floor, and they were rebuking and calling things—rebellion, seduction, manipulation and alcoholism, just to name a few—out of me that I didn't realize were there! I'm still baffled at how easily things can creep into your spirit if you don't guard yourself and cover your life in prayer. That night changed my life forever.

God is so faithful. I know that had it not been for each of those people and Tim, my life would be so different today. But I stand today as a testimony of God's grace and mercy. When the Lord decided enough was enough and gave me deliverance, He totally and complete healed my emotions— even from before I was married.

He healed the emotional damage that was there from thirteen years of sexual abuse by my father, all the way up to the damage I had done to myself during the years of my marriage. God wiped the slate clean. That night I got a brand new start. I was truly restored to God and to my husband. In place of all the bitterness, anger and resentment, the Lord filled me with peace, joy and a brand new love for Tim—a love I didn't know I could have for any man.

Pastor Hubbard, thank you and Patti for being such an awesome man and woman of God. A church is truly a reflection of its pastor. Thank you to our family at United for showing us a pure, godly love that only comes from knowing the heart of God. You were instrumental in the restoration of our marriage. God is good!

Tim Allen: Jesus Is My Reconciler

In October of 1998, my wife Tammy's sin became evident to me. But it wasn't until early 1999 when I found out just how far the sin had taken her. It was a hugely devastating realization.

But what shocked me more was discovering God was more interested in exposing *my* sin. If sin could be measured, mine was the greater, because I was supposed to be the priest of the home standing at the door, guarding my home against the attack of the enemy!

Is there an innocent party when a spouse has an affair? Does the other spouse fall under an "exception clause" or have a right to divorce? My opinion is definitely no on both counts. God's heart is always restoration, and if we give up and throw it all away, Satan wins.

I believe it gives the offended spouse the right only to pray and repent for his or her own sin and pray that God would begin to heal the brokenness in the spouse and in the family. One must begin to cover the spouse and family with prayer, because somewhere there's been a breakdown.

I believe God spoke clearly to me two times during the eighteen months or so that were so difficult after finding out the truth. The first time was when I asked God in my brokenness how it could have happened to me. I was thinking about what a vile person Tammy had to be to do this horrible thing to our family and to me. God's reply was clear and simple: "This happened because of the hardness of your heart." That floored me.

But I'm the innocent party, I thought. I found out later that there is no innocent party in a broken relationship.

The second time God spoke to me I had just secured a lawyer to file for divorce. I felt led to go to the Bible, and as I turned to the first page I grabbed, my eyes fell to the middle of the page. I began to read from Job 5:17, which speaks of the man whom God corrects, but whom He also binds up.

What caught my eye and broke me was how the chapter ended. God's promise is that when all is said and done, you will take inventory of your tent and know that nothing is missing. That told me I had to stay and fight for the family I loved.

God has truly restored not only our family and our marriage, but also our relationship with Him. He is an awesome and merciful God, and He is not done with us yet! I don't believe we can go through a shaking like that and not be used to minister to others.

United Assembly of God Church has been such a vital part of the healing of our marriage. Pastor Whittum gave us unbelievably sound spiritual counsel, and the word that comes from the pulpit each Sunday is truly from God. At the times I needed something but did not know what I needed, the right words came rolling off Pastor Hubbard's lips.

I thank United Assembly of God Church. You are a gift from God to us. I don't know where we would be without this great church and the church family that was vital in our rebuilding. We love you.

Bob Anderson: Jesus Is My Example

As a born-again Christian who has walked with the Lord for almost twenty-five years, I have certain convictions in my heart. I believe that we as Christians ought to form our convictions from God's Word—the Bible. The same is true of the Church. There can be many different opinions about what the Church should be, but if we want to know what God thinks the Church should be, we need to look to the very words of Jesus and the example of the early Church, which had the fresh influence of the earthly presence of Jesus.

The convictions God has put in my heart—the convictions about what Christians ought to be and to do—drew me to United Assembly of God. Similar convictions about what the Church corporately should be and do attracted me and my family to United Assembly of God. After all, we *are* the Church.

Since coming to United, my focus has changed. In the church we attended previously, my focus was on trying to bring emphasis to the things I knew in my heart God was calling us (the Church) to. At United I saw those things happening in abundance.

My focus quickly changed to how we could fit in with all the great things that were happening here, specifically intercessory prayer, evangelism and preaching God's Word in an uncompromising way. At United the message doesn't change, but the methods keep changing. This challenges us to find and use all the resources the Lord has provided for us.

Finally, I am staying at United because, in spite of all the wonderful blessings we have experienced, the leadership is humble enough to realize how far we yet have to go in living and demonstrating the resurrected life.

Diane Baker: Jesus Is My Victory

About three years ago, my life took a turn—not for the good. But at the time I didn't think it was bad.

I had become very unsettled in the church we were attending. I usually went alone (which I hated doing). My son, who was in junior high at the time, was very unhappy in the youth group, and my daughter, who was a senior in high school, and at one time had been very involved in the youth group as a leader, was taking a horrid turn in her own life. She was doing things completely against our morals and everything she had been taught.

I thought I needed to get control over this situation, and since I thought it was caused by something I had done wrong as a parent, I needed to fix it.

One Sunday, as we were driving to church, I asked my husband if we could go to United instead. Both my husband and I came from the churches that had merged in 1973 and had become United Assembly of God. We had many friends at the church, and I just wanted to go there.

Our son reconnected with his old best friend at United and seemed very happy in the youth group. Our daughter was continuing on a downhill spiral, very fast and very dangerously. I still felt as if I needed to have control over her situation, but all I did was make things worse, because with me right in the middle of it, God could not work.

One day I met with Pastor Whittum. I told him how frustrated I was and how scared I was, because I didn't know what was going to happen to her. He challenged me to pray a different prayer. He asked me to pray that "whatever it took," the Lord would bring her back to Himself.

It was not easy to pray that (even though I thought it would be). First of all, I did not know how the Lord would answer my prayer, and second, it meant I had to give up my control over the situation. But I decided to go for it.

My daughter ended up moving out of our home because she didn't like our rules, and she moved in with her boyfriend. I was confused! Why on earth would the Lord answer my prayer like that? But I continued praying. About two months later, she came home—tired, angry, hungry and pregnant.

This was very hard on our family. I was hurt, my husband was angry, and my son was embarrassed. Then I realized God had brought us to United for a very specific reason. We needed these old friends and our new ones. They gathered around us in prayer. They cried with us, and at times when I felt as if I could not pray, they prayed for me. Never did I hear a negative comment, just love. My daughter eventually rededicated her life to the Lord and eighteen months ago brought a precious baby girl into the world.

What I learned most through this is expressed best in Second Chronicles 20:15, 17: "'*Do not be afraid or discouraged because of this vast army. For the battle is not yours, but God's. You will not have to fight this battle. Take up your positions; stand firm and see the deliverance the* LORD *will give you, O Judah and Jerusalem. Do not be afraid; do not be discouraged. Go out to face them tomorrow and the* LORD *will be with you.*'"

Kim Baker: Jesus Is My Protector

As a little girl I grew up loving Jesus with all my heart. I went to a Christian school, was very involved with church functions, and enjoyed spending time doing God's work. But for some reason I still felt alone and out of place.

When I started high school, I was overwhelmed with things I had never been exposed to before. I started smoking and hanging around with the wrong group of people. At sixteen, I started drinking and dabbling in drugs. I kept going downhill, trying something new every so often. By the time I was eighteen, I was heavily involved with clubbing (going to clubs) and with the drug ecstasy.

Still, I knew God loved me. Sometimes, when I was at a club and high on drugs, God would tug at my heart. He reminded me how lucky I was to be alive. With all the alcohol and drugs my body had consumed, I should not have been breathing at that very moment. Yet He was protecting me from my self-destructive way of life. I loved being high, and there was no stopping myself. I ended up moving in with my boyfriend and alienating my entire family.

That was when God showed me His grace in a very unusual way. At the age of eighteen I became pregnant. Strange as it sounds, my pain had just begun. I lost everything—my boyfriend, my friends, my life as I knew it.

My whole world came crashing down in a matter of months. After six years of running from God, I fell at His feet, and nothing has been the same since.

In the midst of all the pain and rejection, I am reminded of God's forgiveness when I look at my little girl. She is the reason I am here today. I am now twenty years old and still being molded. He took me to my very lowest place so that He could rebuild me. I am not ashamed of who I am; I am just so thankful that one day God will use my hurt to heal someone else.

Barbara Belyk: Jesus Is My Encourager

It couldn't have happened at a better time for me to receive the "And Then Some" award, which is given to an individual in my church who works behind the scenes and who goes beyond the call of duty.

I had been married for almost twenty-six years and a Christian for twenty-three of those years. My husband wasn't a Christian then and still isn't. I find that when a person's spouse is not saved, he or she is very limited as to how much they can be involved with church and how much time they can spend there.

When my church first started this program, I was very happy for those who received the award, because I knew they truly deserved it. I also thought I would never receive anything like that because of my situation.

But when I did receive the award that day, it was such a blessing. The Saturday before, my husband and I had just finished the marriage seminar with Gary Smalley. It didn't go as well for us as I had hoped—as a matter of fact, it bombed.

I was really hurting that day. I know I am not worthless in the eyes of the Lord, but the struggle of everyday life with an unsaved spouse can make one feel that way. So, you can just imagine what it did for me personally when I received that award!

I've received other encouragement at my church through the preaching of the Word—I have been damaged but delivered; I am victorious instead of a victim; I can be better instead of bitter; and I am a second "son," just to name a few.

I am so thankful for the ministry at United Assembly of God, even when God is trying to teach me something and the pastor's preaching steps on my toes!

Yvonne Berger: Jesus Is My New Beginning

This past year brought many major changes and challenges for our family. We had attended another church for about twelve years, and after much prayer and seeking the heart of God, we decided to visit United Assembly of God.

Several months later, and after much soul searching, we felt God calling us to make the transition to United. It was not easy, but the timing was very clear to us. The month in which we started attending was "Super September!" It was a wonderful opportunity to see what this church was all about. We loved the spirit and unity that we sensed here.

One evening, about two months after we were at United, after I prayed with our boys and they were in bed for the night, my son, Michael, asked if I noticed that "something is happening to our family." A thrill went through me as I answered yes; I was aware of what he had noticed.

I explained to him that what our family was experiencing was family unity. Many of the principles we were trying to implement in our family were being preached from the pulpit. We were seeing results in the attitudes of our children, and our parental guidance seemed to carry more weight. Our family was in revival! Things were going great.

But sometime in October, my husband, Steve, realized that we were sliding into debt, due to cutbacks at work. His pay had dropped dramatically in the past year, and we were not able to make our bills.

At that time, Pastor Hubbard was teaching about money and exhorting the congregation to use godly principles with what God had provided financially. Steve felt the firm conviction that we needed to sell our home before we got into deep debt. We lived in a beautiful Colonial home, in an unusually close-knit neighborhood. It was the kind of neighborhood where we had block parties, where we borrowed eggs or a can of soup, where we always knew that when we went out to do yard work neighbors would come out to chat. We often had the church youth group over, and we had frequent fund-raiser garage sales. Neighbors came over to donate money or pop cans or whatever. It was heart-wrenching for us to think of moving.

We knew (and kept hearing from the pulpit) that God would provide when we were obedient to what God called us to. But we would rather have been the ones *telling* someone that, instead of the ones *experiencing* it!

We decided to go forward in faith. Our home sold in two months. It was the middle of winter, and we weren't having much success finding a home that met our needs.

We (all six of us) moved into Steve's father's three-bedroom home until we could find a home. It has been extremely difficult, especially for me. It seems as though the Lord has been trying to teach us that our security comes from Him, and it is not things that bring security. It has helped tremendously to hear the pastor's messages of hope and encouragement and of how God allows everything for a purpose.

More than once I felt convicted of having a less than positive attitude. The feeling that this is more than we can bear is being dissolved with the teachings we are receiving. We have taken notes every service, and one Sunday, as we sat in the evening teaching session, Pastor was speaking on Philippians 1:12-16, and God spoke powerfully to us. Steve and I looked at each other and knew that this message was for us.

It will be hard moving into a house half the size of what we used to have, but we are believing that, as at Gilgal, this is a new beginning for our family and that, for some reason, God is calling us back to the basics. We will have to trust in God's purpose for this.

Bill and Bonnie Burger:
Jesus Is Our Marriage Builder

We came to United Assembly of God Church in October of 1999 "poor, blind and naked." Bonnie's coworker, Linda King, had invited us. We were not really looking for a church, but the Missionettes and Royal Rangers sounded like good programs for our children.

We knew we would never regularly attend a church as far away from our home as United (forty-five minutes), but because Linda had diligently searched for churches with these children's programs for us, Bonnie decided to visit.

One Sunday, just the kids and Bonnie went to United while I was at work. Bonnie realized this church is where she wanted to be and that whatever these people had, she wanted it! So on October 17, 1999, Bonnie accepted Jesus into her heart.

Our son, Jacob, didn't like any of the children's programs at churches we had previously visited, so Bonnie was amazed when, as she turned from the altar, she heard him yelling, "Mom, Mom, this is it! We've found the church I want to come to."

On the way home our daughter, Jennifer, began to tell her mom she had learned about the blood of Jesus and how He willingly gave His life so we could have everlasting life. Amazed at this too, Bonnie again realized this was the church for us, but she knew it would take an act of God to get us there because I had said we would never go to a church in Plymouth. We live in Dundee, and Plymouth is too far away!

Bonnie didn't know much about prayer, but she knew she had to talk to God about this. I was a stubborn man with a drinking problem. I knew I could never quit drinking, nor did I want to, so how could I go to church? Despite all this I finally agreed to visit because my wife and kids were so excited about the church—it's all they talked about, constantly!

But it was so foreign to me—people raising their hands and voices, praising God. I thought I could never do that, and why would I want to?

But the people were so nice and genuinely friendly that I continued to come. Shortly after we began visiting, Pastor Hubbard did a series on the family called "It's Raining in My House." Although I would rather have been anywhere but in church, my wife and I both knew we desperately needed a change in our marriage.

After we began to attend Sunday school, Rick and Karen Mattson became our spiritual mentors and friends. Rick and Karen seemed to love us for no apparent reason. We were amazed that a godly couple could have so much love and wisdom for a couple like us in such desperate need of God. They soon became close friends who prayed for us.

God has truly been faithful and merciful in our lives. Our lives were a day-to-day battle. We fought every day over any and everything. It may be hard for some to imagine, but our home was a battlefield, and our innocent children were watching. A threat of divorce often echoed through our raging anger. To say the least, we were a mess but thought this was a normal way of life.

Linda King gave my wife a videotape entitled "Golgotha" (an illustrated sermon preached by Pastor Hubbard) that changed my life. After watching the video on November 4, 1999, I was by myself and feeling alone in the world; then I asked Jesus Christ into my life and my heart.

As I write this, my faith is strengthened because I've taken a few moments and reflected on our Savior's faithfulness, goodness and mercy. Our God is so awesome that by the end of 1999 my marriage was restored, and I was delivered from alcohol. I could go on and on about what God has done in our lives through the faithfulness of Pastor Ken Hubbard.

I am very thankful and grateful to our Lord Jesus Christ and to the church and pastor He has given us.

Jeri Burley: Jesus Is My Reason to Rejoice

My German heritage had instilled in me a stick-to-it grit, a get-it-done stubbornness, a yes-or-no approach to life. For me, life was either black or white, and I believed everybody should like broccoli—period!

So it was hard for me to embrace the dysfunction at United Assembly of God Church during the late 80's and early 90's. My friends and fellow worshipers were leaving the church, yakking, gossiping and dividing us. But my husband and I stuck it out during these bleak years. The spiritual atmosphere was basically one of survival and burnout and without the solid teaching and refreshing we experience now.

At this time, my mother was stricken with a stroke, making it an especially spiritually low time for me. Mom was totally paralyzed on the left side for six years. It was a hard thing to no longer feel the embrace of my mother's arms. I prayed, asking God to heal my mom, and she received the ultimate healing—salvation—and her name was written in the Lamb's Book of Life!

Also during this period of unrest, we adopted a thirteen-year-old child; and I thank God for this blessing. However, as our family adjusted to this change, I felt God was asking me to see life can be "gray," rather than just black and white. God seemed to be telling me it was OK that not everyone liked broccoli.

Things were happening in our home that were foreign to me—rebellion, mistrust, hostility, division, lack of communication, separation, sin—and my rightness became haughiness and self-righteousness. Eventually, I became bitter. Depression set in, and I remember feeling so alone. I put my head on my pillow and cried out, "Jesus, help me."

My German grit helped me stick it out. I thought I was putting on a pretty good façade, but I wasn't. A very good friend said to me, "Jeri, you need help." That offended me, but I decided to let her help me.

Pastor Hubbard came to United around this time. I remember his first sermon. He said, "There are people here that must get rid of bitterness." I thought, *Oh, yeah? I'm right! I have a right to my rightness.* But I heard God say, "Jeri, he's right."

I broke that day, and the healing process began. The "aliveness" of the Word preached by Pastor Hubbard healed my broken spirit.

Now I am leading the prayer ministry at United. I've always been able to talk with Jesus; prayer is a part of who I am. I know God is my Father, and I understand that He hears the cries upon our pillows. And to be trusted by Him and Pastor Hubbard in a leadership position is beyond my ability to reason. But I know that God has mandated it through the authority of Pastor for such a time as this. It's very humbling.

I am grateful for God's trust in me, and I praise Him for His ministry to me and for the restoration of my family. I am thankful that a coworker prayed for me so that, in 1980, I gave in to the goading of the Holy Spirit and accepted Jesus Christ as my Lord and Savior. He washed my sins away and cleansed me from all unrighteousness.

I also thank God that I'm a part of the ministry of our church where people can come and receive the truth. I will rejoice forevermore.

Ed Castro: Jesus Is My Healer

After the Sunday night service, Holy Ghost "car wash" prayer request cards were made available. My prayer requests for physical healing were:

- Healing for my recent knee surgery (I completed physical therapy last week.)
- Pain in my left shoulder (test showed torn ligament; rotator cuff surgery suggested)
- Migraine headaches
- Recurrence of acid reflux disorder

Praise the Lord:

- Doctor specialist advised knee surgery which was successful.
- Specialist believes PT sessions will remedy and heal my shoulder on its own—no surgery!
- Headaches are less frequent; they were caused by caffeine withdrawal.
- Acid reflux episodes are less frequent.

Pastor Hubbard and staff, thank you for your prayers! Also, members of my cell group prayed and laid hands on me. My wife and I are thankful for our home cell group.

Dan and Dawn Divens:
Jesus Is Our Provider

My family and I have been attending United Assembly for almost six years. It has been an incredible time, filled with spiritual, relational and financial blessings. The area we want to briefly focus on is that of finances.

As husband and wife we have put God to the test (see Malachi 3), and He has kept His promises and fulfilled His Word. In so doing, financial blessings in abundance have been ours. God has opened the door for me to change jobs and work for a different company, which ultimately resulted in a one hundred percent pay increase!

In 2001, we agreed to pledge toward the church building program, along with giving our tithe. During that twelve-month period of commitment, I was number one in sales twice. What is even more amazing is that in that same year, my annual income exceeded the previous year by sixteen percent, resulting in my best sales year ever!

When we as Christians waiver in our confidence in God's promises and do not obey His Word, we miss out on His blessings. We often think our pastor, the staff and the church are the ones who receive the blessings from our tithe. The fact is we withhold the blessings of Heaven from ourselves when we choose not to tithe.

Many claim that Jesus did not affirm the tithe. But when asked regarding payment of money to Caesar, Jesus replied, *"Render therefore unto Caesar the things which be Caesar's, and unto God the things which be God's"* (Luke 20:25, KJV).

The Bible declares, *"Give, and it shall be given unto you"* (Luke 6:38 KJV); *"It is more blessed to give than receive"* (Acts 20:35 KJV); and that if we bring all the tithes into God's storehouse, He'll bless our house (Malachi 3:10). When we sow our tithe "seed" into His house and the work of the Kingdom, we have His Word that there will be a harvest and a return on our obedient faith investment. How does our family know this? Because He has kept and confirmed His Word personally in our lives.

"Honour the LORD with all thy substance [wealth], *and with the firstfruits of all thine increase"* (Proverbs 3:9, KJV). If you do, He promises to provide *"all your need according to his riches in glory by Christ Jesus"* (Philippians 4:19, KJV).

Who would you rather have managing your money: Wall Street or the One who created everything we see and experience and who owns it all? *"The earth is the LORD'S, and the fulness thereof; the world, and they that dwell therein"* (Psalm 24:1, KJV).

Test Him! Challenge Him regarding the tithe and your personal finances. See what God will do for His glory and honor!

Debbie Findley:
Jesus Is My Bondage-Breaker

I came to United Assembly of God two years ago. Someone gave me a "ticket" and invited me to a Good Friday sermon. I rededicated my life to the Lord that night.

Before that night my life was a wreck. I was backslidden, living a life of confusion—one foot in the world and the other foot in the Word. I was a believer, but I was bearing no fruit. I was a hearer of the Word, but not a doer of the Word. I had become stained and wrinkled. I was carrying around filthy rags of guilt and bondage. I had lost all my joy, strength and inner peace.

Since Good Friday, 2000, my joy, strength and peace have returned. Pastor Hubbard's teachings have turned my life around. I am a changed person. God has been chipping away at me and tearing down strongholds. I have been set free of bondages that had held me for over twenty years.

In August 2001 I received the baptism of the Holy Spirit. By having God's power through His Spirit in my life, I have felt His presence so strongly. He has empowered me to overcome my fears.

I am forever grateful I went that Good Friday to hear the illustrated sermon that changed my life. I know it was not by accident but by divine appointment that I was there. Now I am involved in home cell ministry and Missionettes. My daughter, Amber, is in Heir Force, and she was baptized on October 7, 2001.

Pastors Bob and Michelle, our children's pastors, have been awesome mentors in her life. She shines when she talks about the love of Jesus. I will be forever grateful to them for teaching my daughter about Jesus. Amber and I are so much happier. We can handle the storms of life with peace in our hearts.

Thank you, United Assembly, for being the "salt" in Plymouth, Michigan. I am forever grateful.

Charlotte Fournier: Jesus Is My Strength

In 1995 I was in a freak accident. I broke my back in two places and fractured my hip and shoulder. I had physical therapy for four years. I went from a walker to a cane and felt as if I was one hundred years old. I was on a lot of strong medication, but nothing helped. I heard that marijuana helped back pain, so I smoked and took pain pills constantly. No one else knew what I was doing.

I grew more depressed every day. With my insurance pending, there was little money coming in. I was a single mother with a daughter who had to grow up really fast. She helped me with my needs around the house, but I was losing everything.

We could not survive on what we had, so I went to the Salvation Army for help. They gave us food and told me a Lutheran church in the area would give me a check for three hundred dollars. I was grateful, but there was a catch. I would have to attend a few classes to hear the Word. So, of course, I did!

I went a few times, but I was angry with God. "Why me, Lord? My life is a wreck." I didn't go back to the classes. I struggled and tried to live my life normally for the next couple of years.

Then one day my daughter came home from school and asked me if she could go to a youth group meeting at United Assembly of God! I told her yes but to be careful! I didn't know what kind of church it was.

When my daughter returned home that night, she was in

awe! She said, "Mom, I think you would like this church," and she asked me to come that Sunday.

I had had enough of churches, but I promised her I would go because she was so happy going there. I wanted to check this place out for my daughter's sake, anyway.

Pastor Hubbard's sermon that day was called "America 911." It was so powerful that I bought the video and came back the next week.

That day, it was as if Pastor Hubbard was talking right to me. "If you live your life in sin, with drugs and addictions, you are a slave to sin. You need Jesus Christ to give you strength," he said.

I cried and said, "That's me!" So I went to the altar and asked God to help me with my pain and addictions. The next day, I woke up with very little pain. I have not had any drugs since that day!

I thank the Lord for my strength and Pastor Hubbard and this congregation, who have enlightened our lives with the Gospel of Jesus Christ.

James Gray: Jesus Is My Deliverer

I gave my life to Jesus on July 26, 1998, in a faith church. Since I was fourteen years old, I had been bound to drugs, depression, violence and sexual immorality. When I got my life right with God, it was as though I could see for the first time. I was delivered and set free!

At that time there was no follow-up or discipleship program at the church, and I had no home church, so I had nowhere to be fed spiritually. When I started going to a Pentecostal church in 1999, I was seeking God and it was awesome! But to me, the church seemed off, doctrinally, and I began wavering between two opinions. I walked around with a huge praise-the-Lord smile on my face, even though I felt I was falling apart on the inside.

A good buddy of mine invited me to visit United Assembly of God to hear the new youth pastor. So I came and immediately knew this was where God wanted me! I attended both Sunday services and listened to Pastor Hubbard speak. God used him to speak directly to me that day.

After I had been attending United for about five months, and was still on seizure medication for epilepsy, I went to the altar to pray for healing. I heard Pastor Hubbard say, "Somebody is getting healed of epilepsy." As soon as he said it, it was as though fire shot through my body!

Later I went back to my doctors, and they said I didn't have a trace of seizures. They said I could get off my medication. I was healed of epilepsy! So I am now living free from any medication or seizures—one hundred percent healed by the Lord!

I placed myself under Pastor Jason's (the youth pastor) mentorship in Holy Hands, which is United's live-in discipleship ministry. Last summer we saw about four hundred people give their lives to Jesus. Now I serve United Assembly of God in the evangelism program under Pastor Jason.

I believe there is no dream worth dreaming if you're not going to keep that dream alive. I also believe that the dream that the Lord has given Pastor Hubbard runs deep, and I love being a part of what God is going to do in my church.

I am now attending Bible college, and I feel the Lord is calling me to full-time ministry. I praise God for allowing me to be a part of His work. I praise God for the work of His Spirit and guidance through my life. And I praise God for the intercessors and pastors from United who have encouraged me through tough spiritual labor and warfare.

Shelby Rae Henley:
Jesus Is My Miracle Worker

(as told by her mother)

On Thursday, April 5, 2001, our daughter, Shelby, age six, was trying to beat her dad and sister out the front door of our house. When she ducked under one branch of a thorn bush, she ducked right into another.

A thorn pierced through the pupil of Shelby's eye. She jumped back and fell on the ground screaming. When her dad and I picked her up, we could see her eye was cloudy white, and the tissue was torn and hanging off. I'm a nurse, so I placed an eye patch over her eye, and we took her to the emergency room.

The ER doctor prescribed antibiotic drops and instructed us to see the eye specialist the next morning. We took her to Dr. Mandell, and upon his examination, he informed us Shelby had had a serious accident and would probably require a cornea transplant in the future. Her eyesight was now 20/400, and she could not see anything.

Dr. Mandell said the thorn had penetrated through Shelby's entire cornea, and she was leaking eye fluid. If all the fluid leaked out, she would lose her eye. Chances of infection were great, and that also put her at risk of losing her eye. Dr. Mandell prescribed some more antibiotic eye drops that needed to be given every hour daily. Also, he instructed us that Shelby would need to be very careful, acting as if she had a fragile egg sitting on her head. Dr. Mandell had to see Shelby every day, including Sunday. He opened his office on Sunday, just to see her.

When we saw Dr. Mandell on Sunday, April 8, 2001, he told us that when we first brought Shelby in the Friday before, he thought her eye would never be spared. He also told us Shelby would never see any better than what it would be like looking through a glass block window. But we knew that people all over the country were praying for her.

He fitted Shelby for a contact that would hold down the scar tissue, which allowed her to see slightly better. Dr. Mandell's aide said that Shelby would always have to wear a contact in that eye.

With each visit to Dr. Mandell's office, Shelby was tested with and without the contact, and with each visit she could see better and better.

On October 1, 2001, Shelby had a regular eye appointment. Dr. Mandell did a special test to show how much of the pupil in Shelby's eye was consumed with scar tissue (which prevents sight). Approximately fifty percent of her pupil was covered by scar tissue.

Then, Dr. Mandell did a regular eye examination without the contact. When he put the letters up on the screen for Shelby to read, starting with larger letters, Shelby got them all correct. He made sure she wasn't cheating by making the letters smaller. Shelby correctly read them again. All the way down to the smallest letters, Shelby could see them.

He asked Shelby, "Are you memorizing these letters? Just to keep you honest, I'm going to switch to numbers." Shelby read all the numbers correctly. She was reading 20/20 without a contact lens and with a full-thickness wound in her eye. Dr. Mandell told us he didn't know how she could see 20/20 with the severity of her injury. He said, "Shelby is a true miracle." It was then I told him we had family and friends all over the United States praying for her.

Shelby will have to see the doctor every year for rechecks, but if you ask her which eye she hurt, she can't even tell you. We know that God healed Shelby's eye completely. Even the doctor said she was a miracle!

Shelby has been praying every night, since about two years old, for the eyesight of Bob Ferguson, a family friend and member of our church. When her eye was damaged, she included herself and Bob's eyes in her bedtime prayers. She still continues to pray for Bob's eyes daily.

Thank God, He does answer prayers.

Keri Horning: Jesus Is My Confidence

I walked into United Assembly of God for the first time in August 2000. I carried a heavy load with me that day. I was a newly graduated educator looking for the perfect job. I had several gut-wrenching interviews at various places. I was desperately looking for connections into any and every school district in the area.

One connection led me to a well-known school district. I met first with one of the principals and then with the board. I thought everything was going well; they liked me, and they seemed very interested. They began to pursue me for an elementary Spanish position. I'd always wanted to become an elementary classroom teacher. This was not exactly what I was looking for, but what other options did I have?

They explained to me that if I would like to continue being considered, I needed to meet with the superintendent and sign some paperwork so the board could look at me further. Naively, I signed the paperwork, not really asking a lot of questions (being twenty-two years old, I didn't realize the importance of doing so). I assumed I would be notified if things were turning out or what the next step would be.

With this in mind, I scoped out other school districts, hoping desperately to find something that fit me better. Surprisingly, I received a call from a school district for which I had filled out an online application. The secretary asked me to fill out the rest of my application online because the principal was very interested in me.

I had never seriously considered this district because it

seemed "out of my league." It was an affluent neighborhood that had more support than one teacher can dream of, not only from administrators and colleagues, but also from parents. Quite honestly, I had not really considered that district to be an option because it seemed as if it was too good to be true.

I met with the principal, and we hit it off from the beginning. She and I talked and "clicked" immediately. I shared with her my student teaching experiences in Detroit, and to my surprise, she had had experience there, too. Everything seemed to click! That school felt like home to me. I walked out, smiling from ear to ear.

Later that week, I was speaking with another prospective teacher from the first district I had applied to, and I asked if she had signed a contract. She said that she hadn't, and I said I hadn't either. Another teacher from that district was standing nearby. He looked at both of us, and in a matter-of-fact tone said, "Both of you already signed contracts. That is what your meeting with the superintendent was for!" My face went white. I got into my car, called my husband, and went into hysterics. What was I going to do?

I had a meeting with the second district later that week, so I called the first district, and without explaining myself, told them I would be unable to fulfill my teaching commitment to them. They told me I was bound to the contract unless someone else could be hired in my place. I felt sick and uneasy for days. What should I do? Should I take legal action against them for taking advantage of me? Wasn't it my own fault for not asking questions?

I met with the second district later that week. I sat in the principal's office for my third interview, this time with an uneasy feeling in the pit of my stomach. I was under obligation to work somewhere else, but I wanted so much to make this wonderful place mine.

That week there were constant phone calls from both districts. The sound of the phone ringing made me feel sick. I didn't want to think about it, but I couldn't get away from it. I was bogged down with worry.

Also that week, my husband and I decided we would check out the church down the street from us. It was an Assembly of God church, the denomination we grew up in. I walked in there that day with a thousand things swirling around my mind, and I wondered if I would be able to concentrate at all. Pastor Whittum began the service with praise and worship, and I felt a little bit better, but that nagging feeling kept pushing on me throughout the worship.

And then it happened. A bald preacher, with a hint of a southern accent and a fire behind his eyes, stepped up to the pulpit. I had no idea what I was in for. He stood on the platform and began to speak.

"I really feel the Lord putting something on my heart right now," he began. I looked up. "There is someone out there who is going through something major in their life. You are at a crossroads, and you are burdened by the weight of what you are carrying around. You are worried all the time, you're not getting rest, you're making yourself sick about this."

I looked down at my shirt, wondering if I had a sign or something on me with the information of my life printed across it. He continued, "The Lord is really impressing upon my heart for you to rest in Him. You need to fully turn it over to Him. You need to stop worrying. Give it to Him. Rest in Him. He will take care of it. Rest in Him."

I went home that day, and I knew I had not only found an answer about what to do about my job situation, but my husband and I made a decision that day regarding what church we would become members of!

I rested in the Lord. I told Him I was going to give it to Him and that I trusted completely what He was going to do with it. No matter what the situation was, I would be OK with it. I received no phone calls for four days. There was finally rest in my home.

I had one final interview with the second district. I knew I would be going in there to meet the superintendent, and I would be signing a contract. I had a strange peace about it. I knew that going in there was the right thing to do, even though I was not technically released from the first district. I signed their contract.

Here is my miracle. The next day I received a letter in the mail from the first district. It was a letter dated two days prior (the day before I signed the second contract), releasing me from the position I had unknowingly signed for. Was it a coincidence that there was no overlap in dates of the contracts? Absolutely not. Was it a coincidence that my husband and I walked into United Assembly that Sunday in August?

As Pastor Hubbard will tell you, "You're not here by accident." That's for sure. I am, needless to say, enjoying my second full year in the district of not even my wildest dreams! And to top it off, we are now members of the greatest church in the whole universe!

> *Be anxious for nothing, but in everything by prayer and supplication, with thanksgiving, let your requests be made known to God; and the peace of God, which surpasses all understanding, will guard your hearts and minds through Christ Jesus.*
>
> Philippians 4:6-7, NKJV

Patti Hubbard: Jesus Is My Transformer

I was raised in a great home. My parents brought me up with good morals and values. They brought me to church every Sunday, so I had a very solid and consistent upbringing. So you say my testimony is…what? Well, even though I had all those positive things in my life, I never came to know the Lord until I was twenty-two years old. My mom and dad did bring me to church, but the only memories I have of church are of the minister smoking during coffee hour, two songs from the hymnal, a fifteen- to twenty-minute sermon, and a few nice people—all in all it was just an hour of religious routine to me. No one ever brought a Bible with them, and I don't recall the minister ever telling us one time how to receive Christ as Savior or even that we needed to. I had a very false perception of God and church and what all that meant.

In my teen years, I entered the party scene. Even though I never felt comfortable at parties, I continued to go and participate in whatever was going on because of the peer pressure. I never seemed to have the courage to say "no." As I approached the age of twenty-two, I got a good job in the insurance field. I was still living at home with my parents and had been dating a boy for about five years. I found myself constantly thinking about trying to become a better person. I was not happy with myself or my lifestyle.

At the place where I was working, there was a new girl just hired named Jackie. We worked closely together and became friends. As I got to know her, I realized she was different. I thought of her as "better" than me. She didn't do the worldly things I did, she never swore like I did, and I could tell there was something special about her life. She was a born-again Christian.

One day when we were talking, she invited me to go with her over lunchtime to a Christian bookstore because she wanted to pick up a Bible study guide. I had never known anyone who had a Bible study guide except the minister, and I never read the Bible. But I told her that I would go with her because I thought I would like learning how to read the Bible. So we made plans to go the next day at lunch.

I drove home later that day and had the house to myself because my parents were away for a few days. When I picked up the mail, I noticed a large manila envelope addressed to *me*. It was from some ministry organization in a different state. I opened it up and couldn't believe my eyes. In the envelope was a free paperback book entitled *The Greatest Love*, along with a letter and pamphlet that said, "Send for your FREE Bible study guide." I just stood there dumb-founded. The only one I had told about my desire to read the Bible was Jackie. I couldn't believe that some ministry I had never heard of had sent me this book.

I was so curious that I sat down right there in a lounge chair outside the house and began reading. The book was a beautiful account of the life of Christ, why He came to earth, why He died, and that we needed to receive Him into our lives. After spending hours reading the book, I felt like a lightbulb had been turned on inside my heart. I went inside, got on my knees and began to cry so deeply. I told God I was so sorry for all the things I had done wrong in my life and that I was going to be a better person. I didn't want to live the way I had been living, and I admitted that I needed Him in my life and His help to change.

It felt like fireworks going off in my living room that night.

Teardrops were all over the carpet. I got up from the floor feeling totally different, totally new. Something wonderful had happened to me! At the time, I couldn't explain it; I just knew it was real. I immediately called Jackie and told her what had happened. She was blown away.

She said, "Patti, you just received Christ in your heart. You're saved—born again!"

I said, "Wow! This is what it feels like to be born again?" I was a completely new person. Everything in my life changed—not in a week, or a month or a year; it was instantly. I felt different and my actions were different from that night on.

The very next day, a woman from my office heard me talking to some others about what had happened to me. She invited me to her church, so that night I went with her to a Wednesday night service at a small Assembly of God church in northeast Grand Rapids. I answered the altar call that evening.

The next day, I broke off the five-year relationship with my boyfriend. I also ended many friendships I had with girlfriends. They thought I had lost my mind. They were telling people I had joined a cult. I began to make new friends at the church, which I had started attending regularly.

As God's presence in my life continued to work in me, my life made a total turnaround and my life's path and future were now in God's hands. Little did I know that the small Assembly of God church I was attending would be the place where I'd meet my future husband (Pastor Ken Hubbard), get married, start ministry, have my first-born child dedicated and much more.... Wow! My life was changed!

Bob Illes: Jesus Is My Anointing

My wife, Michelle, and I started attending United Assembly of God six years ago, and it has been an incredible journey!

Prior to attending United, Michelle and I weren't attending anywhere faithfully. We were discouraged and tired of church. A few of our friends who attended United knew we weren't going to church anywhere and invited us to hear their young preacher. My wife accepted the invitation, but I didn't want to attend anywhere I knew people. I just wanted to blend in with the crowd and be a pew potato!

My wife asked me every week to come, and I finally gave in. I can't tell you what the sermon was about that day, but I could feel the presence of God so strongly! But I fought going to the altar because I guess that's what you do when you are running from the call God has on your life.

In 1987, I was attending North Central Bible College in Minneapolis, Minnesota, and studying to be a youth evangelist. After the year was over, I realized I couldn't afford to go and felt no one believed in me, anyway. So, I gave up my dream of ministry.

Then one Sunday Pastor Hubbard preached a message of healing. He said, "There are things in our past that hinder us from moving forward in God." I realized that the message was for me, and when he gave the altar call, I went down to give everything from my past to God. Pastor Whittum was playing a song about trading our sorrow and shame for the joy of the Lord, and that's exactly what I did! God restored the call on my life.

Pastor Hubbard told me that God was going to use me in a mighty way. He also said something else that meant a lot to me and still does—he told me he believed in me.

God is now using Michelle and me to reach children and parents from all cultural and social backgrounds. God placed a call on my life and gave me a dream of being in ministry. I had given up on that dream, but God hadn't, and when I finally said, "Use me, Lord," He restored that dream.

My wife and I are now the children's pastors at the greatest church in the world.

Deb Koslakiewicz: Jesus Is My Foundation

The Lord works in incredible ways!

My son, Kevin, and his wife, Danielle, invited my husband, Mike, and me to attend United Assembly of God two years ago, and we have been attending ever since. We were backsliders but went forward for the altar call and have since been enjoying the Lord, the church and the ministry.

I don't quite understand everything about it, but I have been blessed with the Holy Spirit. Although I have not been able to speak in tongues, there is a shaking that happens to me, and my hearing has become acute to hearing the answers to certain prayers. I don't pretend to understand it, but I feel as if I'm a support somehow for the pastor, guest speakers and others.

At one time, our daughter-in-law, Danielle, was scheduled to have a lung biopsy because they thought she might have cancer. X-rays showed there were masses on her lungs.

I asked Pastor Hubbard to pray for her, and I admit that at the time I was a little disappointed because he asked me to fill out a prayer card instead. (I was bugging him just minutes before the service was about to begin. But I guess I thought he had better connections with God than I did.) I guess he taught me a lesson that day.

During that service, we had a guest speaker, and for some reason (probably because I was praying so hard for Danielle), the Holy Spirit was making me shake all over.

The speaker was talking about the Holy Spirit at the time and asked people to come to the altar. Mike asked me if I wanted to go forward, but I said I didn't want to. I wanted to go to Danielle, because the Lord was telling me to tell her everything would be fine at the hospital the next day.

I don't like to stand out in a crowd, but that day I didn't feel out of place, and I didn't notice my surroundings. Right in the middle of the church service, I went up to Danielle. I told her God was telling me that everything was going to be fine. The tears were streaming down both our faces.

And Kevin, who I thought would be totally embarrassed by his mother making a spectacle of herself in church, didn't even flinch. In fact, he was sitting in the pew with his eyes closed and didn't even seem to notice us. He told me later that he was having a vision (Kevin had never had a vision before, and I don't think he's had one since). In his vision, God was walking down the hospital corridor; He had one arm around Kevin and one around Danielle.

So the next day, Kevin, Danielle, Mike and I were all very calm at the hospital. Danielle suffers from anxiety attacks, so this was very unusual for her to be so calm. She knew and we all knew that God was in charge and that we had nothing to fear.

And sure enough, the surgeon came out after the surgery to tell us Danielle had no cancer. We know that if she did have it, God had taken it away. Danielle said that during the surgery she was totally at peace because she could feel God's presence. God is so great!

As a side note, Kevin and Danielle have now also been blessed with a beautiful little baby girl. Her name is Emily Grace, and she is the apple of her parents' and grandparents' eyes. We are very grateful to God for all He has done for us.

Brenda Mason: Jesus Is My Delight

One day my oldest daughter, Venus, called me and told me a church was giving away turkeys for Thanksgiving and that they had given one to her and my other daughter, Tomiko.

Venus said they met with the children's pastor named Pastor Bob, and he wanted to sign up their kids for a bike giveaway in December. He told them that all of the kids would get one if they signed up and came in person with their parents to pick it up. The bikes were free. I wondered, *What kind of church is this?*

But the first thing I thought was, *We've got to get these bikes for our kids for Christmas!* We couldn't afford to buy any, so I told my daughter to go to the bike giveaway.

The day of the bike giveaway my grandson, Lydell, was sick and couldn't get his bike. I called one of the pastors, and he said that if I came to the church that Wednesday night he would have a bike there for Lydell. My daughter, Sharina (Lydell's mother), and I ended up going, though we didn't want to.

That night, on the way to church, Sharina and I were talking about what Venus and Tomiko had told us about this being a "white" church. When we arrived, we discovered we were the only people of color there. We looked around for more black people, but we didn't see any.

Before the service we met the pastor, who told us he had the bike and that we could get it after the service. The other people welcomed us in and really "loved on" us before the service. They were so friendly!

When we heard Pastor Hubbard speak, his words pulled

on our hearts. I fell in love with what he was teaching about God. He said that there was no color in God's eyes; God saw only our spirit, and it had no color, so we should treat everyone the same as God does.

After that, Sharina and I decided to come to the eleven o'clock Sunday morning service. (I had been praying for three or four years for God to lead me to a church.)

We got the bike that night, but we really got much more than that. The Lord knew what we needed to hear.

That Sunday, December 30, 1999, we came back, and we gave our hearts to Jesus that day. Also that day, Pastor Hubbard gave everyone a prayer partner. My partner was Karen Monro.

Everything seemed to be going well until the devil found out that I was now God's child. Suddenly everything seemed to be under attack, especially my unsaved husband, Jerry, our son and our finances.

Our problems started with our son. Because of a disagreement with his father, he turned Jerry in for defrauding the government. Police and federal government men were coming to the house, and I was very scared. The fear made me sick to my stomach. I felt like I couldn't go on living another minute.

I waited until my husband went to work each day, and then I would fall on my knees and pray, asking Jesus to help me because I didn't know what to do. I started fasting and praying. I told my prayer partner, and she told me to keep getting closer to God.

On Monday, January 10, 2000, I asked Jerry if I could go to church. By this time, I was going Sundays and Wednesday nights. He said I had been going to church too much, but I told him I just wanted to go that night. He said, "Okay."

A guest speaker, Colleen Heeren, was there that night.

After she spoke, I went to the altar and gave up everything to the Lord that night. I received the Holy Spirit and spoke in tongues. I felt good, as if I could take on the world! I have never felt so much peace in my life. I had a comfort in my heart, and I thanked Jesus for that. I felt as if I had something in my chest that wouldn't let me worry or cry or think on my problems.

But the situation at home was taking a toll on my husband. He wasn't saved, and he tried to kill himself twice. I would fall on my knees and pray for him, and when fear came in, I prayed three or four times a day. When Jerry went to sleep at night, I prayed, and the Holy Spirit would comfort me. My husband told me he felt I was walking around as if nothing was going on. I had such peace (I was dying to self).

Then he tried to kill himself again when the government took all his money, his social security and his pension. They said he would never get it back.

It hurt me so much to see him hurting. I would fall on my knees and ask Jesus to save him so he could have the same peace I had. I prayed and fasted and read my Bible, looking for anything to help him.

Then the court dates started. The thought of jail made him cry. I felt so helpless, because there was nothing I could do for him. So I prayed and prayed. Sometimes the devil would attack me, but I just prayed and fasted more.

On the first court date, Karen Monro and I prayed and prayed. That trial came out well, but that was not the end. They set another trial date. This time they gave Jerry a parole officer, and now my husband was really sick. My prayer partner and I kept praying.

Believe it or not, Jerry and I were blessed again! The trial could have been worse than it was, so I felt we had won the victory.

I kept on praying and getting closer to God; then the devil said, "Well, I'll get you, Brenda! I'll attack your money." (I had just started paying my tithes.) I found out I had lost my social security and insurance. This just tore me apart, and my husband just ran away and cried. We were in fear (which comes from Satan).

One Wednesday night came, and I went to the church service and really listened to the Scripture. I believed in every word. Pastor Hubbard was a blessing, and when I left I was praising God, worshiping Him and loving on Him. I went home and prayed some more. I told God that if I lost everything, whatever I had left, I would give it to Him.

The next morning I got a lawyer. I thank God for His mercy and grace in letting me see what I needed to do. We got a court date in December 2000. I was praying God would give me strength to fight this demon.

I was still suffering through with my husband. I could see his suffering. Sometimes he hurt so bad that I would just fall on my knees and ask God to please have mercy on him. I tried to tell Jerry everything I knew about Jesus so he could find peace.

When the lawyer called, it just tore Jerry up all over again. He told me to leave him alone. "I don't want to hear about your God," he said. It hurt because I knew he couldn't see the spiritual world. All he could see was this world and how we were going to lose everything. The things he told me cut deep inside me. That is why I had to pray.

Sometimes the devil comes and whispers bad things in your ear, trying to steal your joy, such as when my social security papers came. I filled them out, prayed over them, and sent them back. It didn't bother me this time because I had learned to pray about everything and to have faith and let Jesus handle it.

During this time, I joined a cell group that meets once or twice a month. I learned many different things there about the Bible and Jesus and some of the things the others were going through. It was so good to have others to talk to. They taught me how to pray, not only for my family and myself, but also for others.

I learned about trusting in God; I learned about the love of God and how His mercy is new every day; I learned how to spend time with God as my personal Savior. I didn't know I had my own Savior. Now I talked to Him every day as if He was seated in the next chair.

Pastor Hubbard told us that always, no matter what you're feeling, to praise God. So I started praising God everywhere— in the car, in the shower, at the pool or at work, even when I had small attacks. No matter if I felt like it or not, I would remember my pastor saying that God loves praises.

To make a long story short, I won my social security case. Thanks be to God!

Also, my husband was saved in September 2000, thanks to the prayers of church staff and cell groups who pray and share the Lord Jesus Christ. The government took his social security and said he would never get it back. But, thank You, Jesus, we got it back!

We also needed to sell our house. Through a series of miracles from the Lord and with the help of my cell group, we bought a manufactured home for twenty-nine thousand dollars less than the original cost. Oh, the favor of God! Thank You, Lord.

Just when I thought we had finally come through the worst of it all, my mother became ill in February 2001 and ended up in the hospital. The Lord said to me one night, "I want you to go to the hospital and say the sinner's prayer with your mother." I said, "Lord, not me, Lord." I cried, and He said, "Yes, you, today." I knew in my heart I had to do it. I could feel the Holy Spirit pulling me.

I was scared, but the Holy Spirit said I must obey. So I did. I didn't know what to say; I was a new Christian myself. So I had a tape on which the pastor had given the sinner's prayer. I played it over and over and over until I got every word on paper. Then I went to the hospital.

I asked God to help me. I told my mother I would like to pray for her, and she said, "OK." Then I said, "Mom, do you want to give your life to the Lord?" and she said, "Yes." We said the sinner's prayer, and she accepted Jesus as her Lord and Savior.

On May 9, 2001, my mother died. Today I thank God for that day in February when He made me go to the hospital, because today I know where she is. Knowing this was a great comfort, and I made it through her death with the help of my prayer partner, Karen, my cell group and others in the women's ministry.

When times got hard, so many people were there for me, and when I couldn't find my usual prayer partners, Jeri and Mary Grace, the church secretaries, were there to pray with me. The church sent flowers and cards of encouragement. All of this is called "love," and that's what God wants us all to have, one to another—the love of Jesus Christ.

I thank God for United having the bike giveaway. If it hadn't been for this church and its ministry, I would still be lost. But because of United and our pastor, who makes sure we are fed the Word of God, my family and I are washed in the blood of Christ and can stand against the enemy. Thank you, United, for displaying the love of Jesus Christ.

Sharina Mason:
Jesus Is My Faithful Companion

My name is Sharina Mason, and I am a single mother with two boys and a girl, ages fifteen, eleven and ten. I am thirty years old.

I came to United Assembly of God because of a bike giveaway. My two youngest ones received their bikes when they went to United Assembly with their aunt, but my oldest son was sick that day. Later, my mother called the church to see if they had any more bikes. The children's pastor said yes, but we had to come to a service to get it. So my mother and I decided to go that Wednesday to a Bible study.

The plan was to get the bike and run, but when we got there, we found everybody was really nice. But we felt as if we stuck out because we were black, and we thought this was an all-white church.

A bald-headed man stepped up and began the class. After hearing him, I remember thinking, Wow! This guy can preach like a black pastor. He talked about the "land of not enough," "the land of just enough" and "the land of more than enough." At that time in my life, I didn't have anything. I was definitely in "the land of not enough."

After class we got the bike, and Mom and I decided to go the next Sunday because we were so impressed with the pastor.

That December Sunday was the day before the year 1999 ended. Many thought the world would end or something that day.

Pastor Hubbard spoke in the power of the Holy Spirit.

He said, "If the world does come to an end, where will you be?" He was so sure that it was not coming to an end that day and acted as if he didn't care at all if it did. That was what I wanted—to know and make sure, whether it did or didn't, I would be with God. So, on that day I gave my heart to Jesus.

At that time I was dating a guy about eight years younger than I. He had a girlfriend and a baby, but I didn't care. Why should I care? My kids' father's girlfriends didn't care about us, so why should I care about others? It's not my fault she couldn't keep her man satisfied! At that time, that was my heart's condition.

Not that this guy was anything special; I just wanted to use him. I didn't trust him or anyone else. I had a mouth like a sailor, and I drank to get drunk, because even though I had a man, I was still lonely. I began to believe I just didn't need love. I could live without it. Just give me what I needed—sex—and be on your way.

I often left my kids at home alone to go party and would come home drunk. I remember my little son saying, "Are you drunk again?" And he would bring me a bucket.

I thank God for saving me and putting me at United. He knew I needed to be loved just the way I was, and that's what they began to do—they began to love on me. But I knew I was going to have to change. I knew I was going to have to give up the boyfriend. I would call the church thinking I could talk to the pastor about this, but because he has an anointed secretary, she talked to me and prayed for me on the phone every time. And, finally, I let the boyfriend go.

But that didn't stop my mind and my body from waging war on me. It just so happened that Pastor Hubbard was doing a sermon on how the spirit wants the things of God, but the mind and the body are used to doing things their own way. He said, "Which one are you feeding, the mind and body or the spirit?"

He didn't take for granted that everybody knew this. He said, "You're fighting, and you need something. You need to read your Bible, get some worship music, and get some saved friends." He was teaching on exactly what I was going through. I had a problem with trust.

Pastor Hubbard gave an altar call for those who needed a prayer partner, and I got a wonderful lady to pray with me, and she gave me her number.

I know that color doesn't mean anything, but I thought, I can't tell her everything! She's white! A lot of help this will be. But I broke down and called her. She listened and shared things with me she had been through, and she began to help me fight. Even though I didn't tell her exactly what I was dealing with, I was delivered from sexual bondage. I won a battle in the war!

By this time, I was on fire for Jesus. I wanted everybody to know about salvation. I signed up for the training class in evangelism and believed God was going to use me. I had been filled with the Holy Spirit; I was on my way! But God had more work to do.

I thought I could still drink and party as long as I didn't get drunk. Every time I picked up a beer, someone near me whispered to someone else, "There goes Jesus out the window." I know the Lord let me hear this every time it was said.

By this time, Pastor was feeding us the meat of the Word; he wasn't holding anything back. He talked about being carnal and said God was looking for holy people to use. He said Jesus wanted His Body to be a people of holiness and be pleasing to God. I repented that day. I left the drinking and the parties on the altar, and I haven't looked back since.

I still had a problem with loneliness, especially since everything I used to do I didn't do anymore. Then I was invited to a New Year's Eve party at my mother's house with our home cell group. That was one of the best times I've ever had. We were having so much fun that when my sister called, she asked what were we drinking! It was nice to say, "Nothing!" This group made me feel like part of the church, as if I actually belonged.

Pastor Hubbard also spoke to us about a personal relationship with Jesus, talking to Him and spending time with Him, and that's when Jesus began to fill all the lonely places in my heart; He began to heal my heart.

The same men I used to hate I now pray for. The same women that didn't care about my kids and me, I now have a heart for, and I pray for them daily.

Jesus became my everything—my Husband, my children's Father, and my Provider. I know God is going to use me to help deliver some other single women and mothers from this curse, which is a stronghold in our nation.

Karen Monro: Jesus Is My Curse-Breaker

Glory to the Lord because He has healed and is continuing to heal the holes in my life. I am grateful beyond words.

I was given away as a baby by my fourteen-year-old birth mother. I was placed in an orphanage, until six months later when I was adopted by an older couple. My adoptive mom's purpose in adopting me was to save her marriage. Unfortunately, it didn't work, and my father walked out when I was three years old.

When I turned five, my mother remarried. Shortly after her marriage to my stepfather, they adopted a sister "for me." Mom deserted us emotionally when I was seven by taking to her bed for days, weeks and months at a time. It then became my responsibility to run the household.

I saw my adoptive father monthly as a young child and then sporadically as I entered my teens. However, when I turned fourteen, he began treating me in inappropriate ways, and I avoided him for great stretches of time. I believe that in his mind he thought it was okay, because I was adopted and not his "real" daughter.

From my earliest memories, I always knew I was adopted, and my mother took great pains to instruct me in the circumstances of my birth. She also let me know that she believed I would undoubtedly also be pregnant by the time I was fourteen.

I was so desperate to get away from both her and my stepfather that I convinced her to allow me to marry at sixteen. The marriage lasted ten months, and then I was back home. I immediately went looking for someone else and managed to get pregnant and married again at seventeen.

We had two beautiful children over the next few years, but our marriage was not in wonderful shape. My husband convinced me that what we needed was another child. When I was twenty-five and four months pregnant with that child, he fell in love with someone else, and he left.

I got a job three days after I gave birth to my youngest child and managed to get by for three years. Close to the end of that time, the new man in my life, whom I thought I loved and that I was certain would be my next husband, beat me badly.

I spent a week in the hospital and some time out of work recuperating. At that point, my ex-husband and his new wife approached me. He said he missed having the children around. He wanted to take them for the summer and then possibly keep them; I would have them on weekends.

They spoke to me about the benefits to the children of having a full-time mother at home, as well as a father in the house. They also spoke about the fact they could afford so much more than I could.

I saw benefits for my children that I couldn't give them. The dark side is that I also saw benefits for me. Yes, I was tired—but there were other reasons that were just as compelling. They were talking to a woman who had never truly had a childhood and who was never free from responsibility.

So, I did give it a great deal of thought, and ultimately bought my freedom by sending my children to live with their father. I regretted it after the first six months they were gone but was too weak to do anything about it. They were with their father for six years, and when they began to run away from his home, I finally stood up, and they came back to me.

Things weren't easy after the children came back to live with me. Those were bad economic times, and my ex-husband wasn't able to provide any child support. There were a number of times I worked three jobs. There were times we were hungry. Kind people brought us food, even though we didn't attend their church—or any church.

Off and on during that period, I went to school at night. At this point, my son was lost to drugs and alcohol. At nineteen, he moved to Ohio to get away from the people he knew in this area. My older daughter married at seventeen and then became pregnant with my first grandchild.

As the world came crashing down around my ears, the bank foreclosed on my house, and my younger daughter had to move back in with her dad for six months until I could find us a place to live. But despite all of that pain and trial, my children and I built something together, and love has survived.

Then, in 1994, the Lord reached into my life and showed me the path to salvation. I grabbed onto it like a dying woman, because that's what I was. He has since healed so many things in my life—an addiction to smoking, a nasty tongue, a foul temper, and that is just the small stuff. He's still working on me. My son and I are saved, and I know that ultimately my daughters will join us.

In 1999, after joining United Assembly of God, Pastor Hubbard invited Sean Smith to speak to us one Sunday. That night he spoke healing over a number of people. I will never forget that night.

I was wearing a pink sweater and sitting halfway back in the pews. I had my eyes closed and was praying when I heard Sean call the woman in pink to step out into the aisle. I started praying that God would touch this woman, whoever she was. It never occurred to me that he could be speaking to me because I hardly knew anyone in the church at this point. Of course that didn't matter to God because He knew I was there. Speaking through Sean, God identified my suffering through attacks of depression throughout my adult life. Sean asked if I wanted to be healed, and I immediately answered yes! He told me to take a deep breath; God was healing me. I actually felt God's healing touch come over me.

That's why the feelings I started having in April of 1999 were a mystery. They didn't feel like what I remembered as depression, yet every time I entered the church I began to cry. In the business world I was taught that crying was a sign of weakness, so I learned to detest tears, particularly my own, and was embarrassed by them. As a result, each week I moved closer to the back of the church until there was no place left to go but out the door.

I knew that I needed to talk to someone about this problem, so I made an appointment to see Pastor Hubbard. I don't remember a lot of what was said that day. We talked about a number of things. Pastor Hubbard talked—I just blubbered. But one thing he said hit me like a lightning bolt. It was such a simple statement, but it was like being given the key to the city! He told me:

> *When everything in you is feeling bad and you just want to run away from life — and also from God — that's the exact moment that you should turn and run into God's arms. The feelings of retreat are not from Him. He would never tell you to turn away from Himself. That's the very time that He is standing there waiting to be allowed to comfort you, to console you, to help you through your struggle and to forgive you.*

God began the healing process in me, but the enemy that wants to rob, kill and destroy was truly defeated by the knowledge given me by Pastor Hubbard that day in early May. That truth is now the base of my Christian walk. When my feelings say "Run, hide, escape," my mind remembers to say "Go ahead and run—but run to God, hide in His arms, escape to His presence."

Six months later, Pastor Hubbard spoke a prophecy over me that I would become the spiritual mother to many young people. In the summer of 2000, God faithfully guided me to complete a forty-day fast, and in the fall of that year, I was honored to lead eighteen teenagers and eleven adults to "The Call," a Christian youth event, in Washington, D.C. I participated in the Impact Youth Ministry for a year and a half.

In 2000, I was also asked to apprentice as a lay pastor in the Mattsons' home cell group. Our group had multiplied by the end of 2001, and I took over my own group as a lay pastor.

But the Lord never stops working in our lives, thank God. I have been going through trials at work for the past year and a half. I did not respond to those trials in what I now know is the appropriate manner. Unfortunately, you don't get a "do-over" in life, but isn't it just like our God to take what the devil meant for bad and turn it to good!

God has used this period in my life to bring me to a point where I could recognize I've lived my whole life in my own strength and prided myself on it.

My past experiences had taught me that the only one I could depend on was myself, and that the only one I could trust was myself. If someone had asked me a year ago if I trusted God, I would have responded, "Of course I do." But God knew differently.

I thought I was whole and together, and even through this whole job situation (which I'm still working through) I continued doing it on my own. In the summer of 2001, God said, "Enough!"

On July 14 of that summer, Pastor Hubbard preached a message called "The Night Time Is the Right Time." That was the day God chose to break the remaining spiritual bondages in my life.

The healing process is ongoing, and God is continuing to reveal new things to my heart. I feel Him daily—yes, I mean I actually feel His presence. Thank You, Lord. I now know that I know that I know He will never leave or forsake me. I don't just know the words, I actually know He is in charge of my life, and He has a good plan for me.

He has given me His joy. He has sent me ministering angels—Karen Mattson, Jeri Burley and Bonnie Burger During the rough period before the breaking, they listened to me and loved on me as the poison worked its way out of my system. They force-fed me love. They wouldn't let me run.

The Lord didn't just show me that I could trust Him. He showed me that there are others I can trust—people that won't walk away when the going gets rough.

I'm especially thankful to Pastor Hubbard. I know that even without him, God would have found a way to do His work in me, but He didn't have to find another way because He had His obedient servant Ken Hubbard to speak through and to accomplish those things. I thank God for all Pastor Hubbard continues to do for us in obedience to God's call on his life.

Dan Morgan: Jesus Is My Enabler

The Morgan family first came to United Assembly of God seven years ago, in May 1995. The only explanation I can give as to why we came to United, much less why we stayed, is God. United didn't exactly have a great reputation for being a dynamic, growing church at that time.

In fact, there was no pastor the first Sunday we attended, and there were only about eighty people in the congregation. There didn't appear to be anything there that would bring us back—except for one thing: God spoke to me very clearly and told me this is where we needed to be.

A lot has transpired in the past seven years. But to clearly understand how God has used this church and ministry to affect our family, one needs to understand where we were compared to where we are.

I was dedicated to and attended the Assemblies of God all of my life, and so had both of my sons. My wife was saved and had been attending church for over twenty years. We were all saved and on our way to Heaven, but the path we were taking to get there was not according to God's plan.

The previous ten years we had attended three different churches. Our involvement in those churches was minimal, and my own personal ministry was nonexistent. Church had become a chore, and it was easy to find excuses not to go. The groove we were in when we first got saved had turned into a rut. I remember my mindset at that time was to not get too involved or too close to God because He may ask something of me.

Since that time, God has used Pastor Hubbard to show

us just how practical and relevant the Gospel is to our daily lives. Everyone in our family now enjoys coming to church. All of us have either been filled with the Holy Spirit or are seeking the baptism of the Holy Spirit, and all of us are involved in ministry.

I could never have imagined that God would ever use us as lay pastors or in the marriage ministry. I could never have imagined that I would have spoken about prayer to the congregation on a Wednesday night. I just didn't think I had it in me to do those things. The truth is, I didn't have it in me, and I still don't. But God in me has enabled my family and me to serve Him.

Looking back to that Sunday in May seven years ago, I can now see why God, against my better judgment, wanted us to stay at United. We still have a lot of growing to do, and God is certainly not done with us. But it's good to know that even though we get off course from time to time, God still has us headed in the right direction.

The past is the past, and I'm enjoying the present and all of the things that God is doing at United. But even more than that, I look forward to the future and all of the things that God has in store for us.

Wolfgang Mueller: Jesus Is My Intercessor

I have prayed a great deal recently for the ability to convey, in words, the enormous magnitude of God's presence in my family's life. My son, Wolfgang Steele, was born a healthy eight pounds, five ounces, on July 28, 2001. That he even made it to that beautiful day is truly a miracle, the culmination of a series of little miracles.

My wife, Shanna, and I were fortunate to announce her pregnancy after resorting to in vitro fertilization. Because of her age, the doctors performed an amniocentesis procedure at sixteen weeks. Two days later, we were devastated when the doctors called to say that our baby tested positive for trisomy 21, or Down syndrome, a condition resulting from an extra chromosome at the twenty-first pair.

The doctors discussed with us the myriad physical and developmental deficits that could occur, including mental retardation, heart and intestinal defects, and physical abnormalities. They suggested termination of the pregnancy as an option. We never considered that option but prayed for guidance to be able to accept our new situation.

That weekend, we saw an uplifting music video by singer Garth Brooks that dealt with a young man who was born with Down syndrome. We haven't seen the video since, but it was the right sign at the right time for us. We considered it an answer to our prayers.

From that day forward, we couldn't wait for the arrival of our special child, especially knowing we would have the great support of our pastor, Ken Hubbard, and other church members who were aware of our situation. We also received a tremendous amount of support and prayer from Pastor Geraldine Richardson of our extended church family in my mother-in-law's hometown.

At the six-and-one-half-month mark, we were concerned about my wife's appearance because her stomach looked like she was about to give birth to triplets any day.

One day, my wife's best friend, Angela, was getting her hair done at a salon she hadn't visited in years. The owner of the salon overheard Angela telling the stylist about Shanna and the baby's condition. He followed Angela out to her car and told her he had several salons and hardly ever went to that one. However, he had felt the need to go to that particular salon that day because he knew he was needed but didn't know why until he heard her talk about Shanna.

He insisted that Angela bring my wife to his church so that the pastor could lay his hands on her, as he was well known for his gift of healing. He said he would tell the pastor in advance.

On that Sunday, we went with Angela to the church, hoping to talk to the pastor and have him pray over her. At the end of the service, the pastor began walking through the church and called Shanna to the altar. He laid hands on my wife and told her everything would be fine with the baby. However, it wasn't until days later that we learned the salon owner had not been able to make it to the church and had not talked to the pastor before the service. The pastor had simply identified Shanna as someone in need of healing.

Three days later, while she was in the hospital for a routine ultrasound, the doctors told my wife she would need to be hospitalized immediately. Our son had developed a condition called fetal hydrops, a condition that causes excessive fluid buildup around the heart, lungs and brain, as well as within the skin.

The ultrasound images clearly showed something was seriously wrong. Additionally, the tests showed my wife had four inches of fluid between the baby and her uterine wall: hence the appearance of triplets. I began to research the condition, which led to the conclusion that fetal hydrops results in one hundred percent mortality in a fetus, due to congestive organ failure. This was confirmed by the reaction of the doctors, who again suggested termination of the pregnancy as an option. The doctors obviously had not considered the power of prayer and God's ultimate will!

Although we were devastated by this horrible development, we gathered family and friends for daily prayer. We also had several pastors and churches praying for us.

I was drawn to Matthew 18:19, in which Jesus states, *"Again, I tell you that if two of you on earth agree about anything you ask for, it will be done for you by my Father in heaven. For where two or three come together in my name, there I am with them."*

A family member who is married to a pastor also enlightened us by demonstrating how the Bible describes the purifying, cleansing power of water. We firmly believed that God was using the fluid buildup to cleanse our child of the conditions that afflict children with Down syndrome. Despite the increasing fluid buildup around his heart and lungs, our unborn child was fighting and showing a strong heartbeat.

Shanna was hospitalized for about three weeks, and we came to know firsthand the ways in which God works through people. One afternoon, she was in a great deal of pain, much more than usual. The pain was accompanied by a great burning sensation radiating throughout her midsection. She was doubled over in pain, and I was helpless to do anything but comfort her and give her a cold compress.

Suddenly, a woman whose job was to deliver water to patients on the maternity ward came to our room. She saw what was transpiring and immediately began to pray. She even kicked out the nurse who had arrived, telling her that if she didn't know how to pray, she had to leave.

The woman began to lay hands on my wife and started speaking in tongues. After about seven minutes of fervent prayer, the burning feeling began to subside, and the pain lessened somewhat. We were grateful for the woman's prayer but were not prepared for what was to come.

During Shanna's entire stay at the hospital, she had to undergo daily ultrasound tests to monitor our baby's condition. Day after day, the monitor showed excess fluid around the major organs and throughout his skin. However, as Shanna was undergoing her ultrasound exam the day after the woman laid hands on her and spoke in tongues, doctors and nurses began scrambling in and out of the room, all viewing the monitor and scratching their heads. The fluid around our child's organs and throughout his skin had completely disappeared!

The doctors could not explain how it happened, as they had no explanation for its occurrence in the first place. We told the doctors and nurses that it was God's miracle and that we wanted it noted in the medical records. Amazingly, the excess fluid in my wife's womb also returned to normal levels within two days. She was released from the hospital within a week and gave birth to our son five weeks later.

Little Wolfie turned ten months old this week. He has suffered none of the physical or developmental deficits that are hallmarks of children with Down syndrome. Chromosome tests have verified that he still has trisomy 21. Wolfie is a happy, beautiful child who has amazed the professionals who work with Down syndrome children. We simply tell them our story to let them know there is a reason for the miracle.

I have come to realize several things as a result of this

experience. First, I believe that God challenges each of us but equips us with the tools to overcome any obstacles. He tested the strength of our faith throughout this experience, especially when we learned of the fetal hydrops only three days after the pastor laid hands on my wife.

Perhaps He wanted to see how we would react after being elated by the pastor's words just a few days earlier, since it is easy to have faith when things are going well.

Second, I also realize that God uses people from all walks of life to accomplish His purpose. Though we had pastors and other church members praying for us when Shanna was in her greatest pain, a woman who delivers water helped rid her of it by laying hands on her and speaking in tongues. Was it coincidence that the very next day the fetal hydrops condition was gone? I think not. I believe it was God using a humble servant to carry out His work.

I tell this story to help those who may be confused or who doubt God's power to heal all our ills, of whatever nature. So often we hear of miracles occurring to people "out there" and wish that one would happen to us. My son is living proof that miracles happen right in our midst and that we simply need to lift our voices and arms and pray.

I have never asked why this happened to us (as if God actually owes me an explanation!). I simply relied on my faith even more when things looked darkest.

I have been saved only three years, yet I know God has made a huge difference in my life. Our son's life is but one beautiful example.

Nick Pagano:
Jesus Is Our Freedom From Debt

As I write this note, we are debt free with the exception of our home. It has not always been this way, and I'd like to share some of our journey and the lessons that we have learned, which may bless other people.

My wife and I were speaking to a group in Texas recently, and as we shared a little of our story, I heard a number of gasps from the audience. I interpreted them as gasps of unbelief. I found out later that they were actually gasps of empathy because a number of people had been through very similar situations.

Approximately ten years ago, I was laid off my job, and as I discussed the future possibilities with Janice, my wife, we decided that it might be a good time for me to pursue owning my own company. I have a great deal of ambition and financial drive, and we thought God would bless our business. (Lesson learned at the time: I admit I was not faithful with my tithe.)

The business started out okay, but after a short time, I was approached by a gentleman (who was not from my church) to investigate my need for a partner. Given that he was a Christian lawyer, I thought partnering with him might be a good opportunity. To make a long story short, he walked out on the company and me after poisoning the employees toward me and taking the money from the bank. (Lesson learned: Janice didn't trust him from the moment she met him. God does give people in your life to protect you if you will listen to them.)

It was a low point in our lives. Our finances were a mess. Actually, they didn't even exist. I decided not to tell Janice about the depth of our debt in an effort to protect her. What I didn't know was that she was getting calls from bill collectors and was more aware of our financial turmoil than I was. (Lesson learned: Full disclosure is a better policy, because God cannot bless deceit.)

I was forced to face my own weaknesses and my own priorities in an attempt to put our lives back together. I was embarrassed by my business failure and mad at God for "causing" it. (Lessons learned: First, God will humble you at the point of your human strength. Second, failing in an effort or a project is not a really a failure, because every success must be preceded by failing.)

The journey has taught us much more than I have expressed in this short note. I am continually reflecting on Pastor Hubbard's sermon that man has a choice about living: He can live a life of survival, live a life of success, or live a life of significance.

Had I not gone through this experience, I know I would have had a difficult, if not impossible, time relating to people who are struggling financially. Now I know that helping these people is my gift to the Body of Christ, and I am looking forward to serving God with it more and more in the future.

Jeff Pasquale: Jesus Is My Reason for Living

Try to picture where you would be and what your life would be like without Jesus. For over sixteen years of my life I tried to do things on my own. I told myself that just being a good person was all there was to life and serving Jesus was not really needed. But I soon discovered that living a life without Jesus and just existing is no life at all. What good is a fruit tree that never bears any fruit?

I was living day to day trying to find something to fill the huge void in my life. I tried various jobs, thinking money was going to help, but it didn't. Partying every night wasn't the answer, either. Everything I tried, and everywhere I looked, I found the reality of the situation was that on my own I was not going to find what I needed.

Once this awareness set upon me, I started feeling depressed. Depression is like cancer, and if you let it go untreated, the enemy will use it to destroy you. When God places a call on your life and you stop fulfilling that call and open yourself up to the enemy, he will march right in and do whatever he needs to do to destroy you. The weapon the devil used on me was depression.

I looked into a mirror and did not like what I saw. My life was a failure. *Who cares if I live or die?* I wondered. With no regard for my family or anyone else, I drove to the airport and bought a one-way ticket to Las Vegas with the sole intent of killing myself. Only because of the prayers of family and friends, which brought about divine intervention, were my suicide attempts unsuccessful. Being in dire straits, I called home and told my mom I wanted to die and had just called to tell her goodbye.

The next thing I knew the phone rang, and it was my sister-in-law Jennifer calling from Louisiana. How did she find me? You'll have to ask God that question. We talked for a while, and she prayed with me and told me that there are people who love me and care about me.

Soon my brother, Rick, was there with me in the hotel and escorted me back to Michigan where I was placed in the psychiatric ward at St. Joseph's Hospital in Ann Arbor. After my release from the hospital, I went to a type of half-way house, to try to make the adjustment back into society. During this time, I was taking medication and going to therapy. Two weeks later, I was released and sent home to live on my own. My first night at home I took about forty sleeping pills and tried to end it all.

Realizing what I had done, I picked up the phone and called 911, asking for help. Truly, there was a part of me that didn't want to die. I was taken to St. Joseph's again, where they pumped my stomach and then transferred me to the University of Michigan Hospital psychiatric ward. My first night there I called home, and my father answered the phone. I told him where I was and what was going on.

My father prayed with me over the phone, and while he was praying, it was as if Jesus appeared next to me, put His arm around me, and said, "Jeff, I'm here for you, and I love you and will be your friend." The feeling that came over me then was something I hadn't felt in a long time; the joy, the exhilaration was overwhelming. The dark cloud that hung over my head was gone, and the sunlight was so bright I needed two pairs of sunglasses!

All this time, through the pain, through the misery, I

thought no one cared about me and my life didn't matter, but Jesus was with me. Satan had blinded me to where I couldn't see Jesus. I thought the doctors could help with their medicine and therapy—they didn't. Not until I allowed Jesus to take over did my recovery start. So if you feel like I did or can relate to any of my predicaments, then I can tell you that only Jesus can help, and all you have to do is ask.

There are a couple of things I'd like to share: Jesus loves you and would still have died on the cross if you were the only one on earth, and your salvation is not just for you, but for others. You have been given a gift that was meant to be shared.

Jennifer Pasquale: Jesus Is My Milestone

For me, knowing who I am is directly related to understanding who God is. I truly started that understanding process at the age of fifteen. My mother, who was thirty-nine at the time, was killed by a drunk driver the summer of my fifteenth year. It was a devastating loss in my life. She had been my best friend, my confidante and my guide.

I can remember thinking, *"Now what will I do?"* I discovered my mother's worn red leather Bible in the drawer of her dresser. In the flyleaf, she had written this familiar prayer: "God, grant me the serenity to accept the things I cannot change, the courage to change the things I can, and the wisdom to know the difference." It was time for me to accept a devastating tragedy and use the courage lessons I had learned to change the tragedy into triumph.

You see, throughout my life I had been learning about God, but my faith had not really been put to the test yet. I had memorized scriptures, but the impact they would have on my life was a process of integrating knowledge with emotion or facts with feelings. I had lots of facts, but now I had emotions and feelings that did not "compute." Fear gripped me so tightly that it felt as if my heart was exploding inside. The sadness was so overwhelming that I can remember being curled up in the fetal position in the corner of the bathroom, sobbing for hours. How do you come to terms with the image of a loving God in the face of such unfair and cruel circumstances?

There have been other major events in my life that have caused me to question this puzzle of life and all the pieces lying there. When I had two ruptured discs and a bone fusion operation, an artery was cut in my neck and I was literally bleeding to death. My life hung in the balance as I lay in Intensive Care for three days totally unaware of what was happening.

I've seen my precious father diagnosed with stage-four cancer, and watched as his faith gave all of us courage to keep going. And I've seen God heal that same man.

I've endured disappointments too painful to write about, and yet experienced the loving arms of God wrapped around me in such a way that His presence was tangible to me. I've felt His touch in moments of quiet prayer, and I've sensed His love in times of desperate conversations between Him and me.

I have been guided by God's Word so many times it would take hundreds of books to record it all. His Word has truly been a lamp to my often-disabled feet and a light to my broken and distorted path. I have come to the conclusion that He is an awesome God in the midst of an awful world and that He is the "wind beneath my wings" and the healer of my broken wings.

I wrote in my book, *Memories and Milestones,* those memories that gave me the strength and encouragement to step forward in life. Some of those memories remind me that life doesn't have to be perfect to find joy in it. I've learned through my life's deep adversities that Christ is the creator of my character. In times of trouble, He was allowing my character to be developed by eternity's guidelines. God did not kill my mother—that drunk driver did. But God stayed close by me when my mother's death, and other "stuff," happened in order to see me through those things.

I'm learning, even from recent events, that I am in a life-long process of realizing that a crisis can bring out the best and worst in a person. Many times I feel totally insecure in what surrounds me, but I continue to stand on God's promises in His Word, not always because I feel confident, but because He tells me to.

Everyone goes through experiences in life that require a recovery period. What we do in the recovery process is up to us. Through the crises in my life, I have learned to respond to God and not to circumstance. Yes, my feelings surface more than they should, but my Comforter understands that. If Jesus could still a storm on the Sea of Galilee, then I can trust Him to speak "peace" to my storms as they come along. Because of a few "hail stones" in my life, I have reached new milestones in my life, and I keep stepping forward with each one.

Someday, when I meet Him face-to-face, I will stand with head held high shoulders back and with confidence in my heart that I have fought a good fight and have finished my race. He will say to me, "Well done, good and faithful servant; enter into your rest." I can't wait for that day!

Bonnie Pearce:
Jesus Is My Ever-present Guide

I grew up in a Christian home, but all that really meant was that I knew about God. I spent most of my life struggling with anorexia, which was what drew me away from church in the beginning. I didn't want to give my life to God; I wanted to live it how I wanted.

I wanted nothing more than to have that "picture perfect image." I spent all of my time exercising and striving to be the best. I would make ridiculous goals for myself, like not eating for forty days. And when I failed, I would become so depressed that I couldn't stand myself, so I would binge on food and then throw up.

I hated myself so much; I hated who God had made me to be. I blamed God for my problems. It didn't matter to me that everyone around me told me that I was beautiful; I didn't feel it inside. To me, the image in my mirror looked horrible. I could only see this girl with a big, round face, fat arms and practically nothing right about her. I couldn't look into my mirror without crying.

My mind was so consumed with how I looked that I wouldn't leave my house. I was afraid to go jogging in case anyone would see me and think that I should be jogging even harder because I was so fat.

My goals became nightmares. I wouldn't allow myself to sleep because I believed that if I stayed up at night I would burn more calories. I would eventually become so weak that I couldn't do anything. I started having anxiety attacks where I would curl up in a ball and cry uncontrollably.

My relationships with my friends were terrible. I would sometimes lose control and start screaming at whoever was with me and then storm out the door, or I would take innocent pieces of conversation the wrong way and start an argument. I went through friends as though they were disposable, as though they didn't matter, and eventually I ended up with friends who were into doing drugs.

Drugs quickly became my escape from the reality that I hated to face so much. I began taking large quantities of prescription pills. Soon my life became one big party. The relief that the drugs gave me from my anxieties was so great that I learned to love life as long as I was on the pills.

I felt better about myself when I was on the drugs, and my life became one party after another. I began getting high every day after school or after work. Soon I was smoking pot. Because the friends I had didn't do illegal drugs, I stopped hanging with them and began to collect new friends who were into the harder drugs.

Eventually I got into ecstasy. I would spend all my money on ecstasy and cigarettes. I ended up doing the drug so much that even my friends told me I needed to cut back. That's how out of control my life was getting.

My life at home with my parents was in bad shape by this time. I had started staying overnight with friends or staying away from home altogether just to avoid my parents. When I was there, we did nothing but argue, and they would want to drug test me.

School became my hideout from my parents, but eventually my teachers began to suspect my drug use too. I wanted to drop out, but I knew my parents would never let me, so I told them and the school counselor that I wanted to transfer to an alternative school the next semester. They let me drop out of the school I was in, believing I was going to start the other school when the next semester began. I had no real intentions of ever following through with that.

I got a full-time job during this time and began blowing my entire paycheck on drugs. Usually the paycheck would be gone by the time the weekend was over and I would have to go the whole week without any money. When the next school semester came, my parents got me into an alternative school in spite of my original plan not to go at all.

I loved school there because we would take smoking breaks off campus, and practically everyone smoked weed. I was eventually off the ecstasy, but smoking weed all the time.

One day my parents came up to school to get some papers they needed out of the trunk of the car that I leased from my dad. The car reeked of weed, so they searched it and found my stash. My dad pulled me out of that school and took me home. I was so angry with them that I packed my stuff and moved in with a friend and her family. Even though her parents were cool, I felt like a burden there, and I was depressed and miserable.

Soon I graduated and started a full-time job. I moved out of Sarah's house and in with another friend who had her own place. For once there were no rules. I could come and go as I pleased, but that soon became a nightmare. There were a lot of hard drugs in that area, and I soon found myself addicted to cocaine. I was spending two hundred to three hundred dollars a day on cocaine. I was deep into debt with my bank.

I lost so much weight that I dropped down to one hundred pounds. There were several times that I almost overdosed, but God stepped in and kept it from happening. I know now that God saved my life many times. Even though I hated God, He was still there for me.

My dad found out about my debts and told me that he would pay off the bank for me and that I could repay him. My parents met me at the bank, and then we went out to eat afterward.

At lunch, my parents began talking about the church service and said it was so awesome that I should check it out. I figured I didn't have anything better to do, so I went to the next service.

I cried through the entire service. I tried fighting back the tears because I didn't want to look pathetic, but I couldn't help it. What the speaker had to say really hit me right where I needed to be hit. I didn't go to the altar, but I did spend a long time afterward in Pastor Jay's office, where I finally gave my life to God.

That day changed my life forever. I didn't become perfect overnight, but Pastor Jay spent time on the phone with me practically every day, helping me understand God's love for me.

I struggled so much and still do to this day. Giving my life to God has not been easy. It's been the hardest thing in my life. There were so many days, at first, that I felt so unloved, but God was always there, and He would send someone my way to let me know that He loves me.

There have been so many people in my life that I would not have made it without them. Pastor Jay is just one of many. I had, and still have, a lot of junk that I have to deal with, but I now know that God is on my side. God has totally healed me from anorexia. It didn't happen overnight, but it did happen. And with God's help, I've been able to stay off drugs, something I never thought was possible.

God has brought me through a past that only comes back in my darkest of dreams. He is now taking me to a new level, and I know He has a calling on my life. I want everyone to know that there is a loving God and that He will take them in His arms and heal them of all their past hurts. If it weren't for God, I know that I would be dead by now. My old friends have tried to tell me that there is no God, but I know there is. I am living proof that He exists.

Skip Presnell: Jesus Is My Redeemer

I really don't know what the problems were in my life when I was a little kid. I don't know what made me as mean as I was. But as early as I can remember, I really didn't like anybody or anything. Even as a young kid at five or six, I was always beating up on people. I was just outright mean.

As I got older, I just got meaner, and my parents sent me to an all boys' alternative school, which was a place where they teach kids who are "slow" and really messed up. I knew it wasn't for me. They even told my parents, "We can't teach him anything; he has it set in his mind that he's not going to learn." And I wouldn't!

At twelve, I can remember my mom taking me to another place. The first day I was there, a kid ran up and punched me in the face. Mom left me there, and after she left, I was taken downstairs to the gym. About thirty kids attacked me and beat me up pretty badly. They spit on me, kicked me in the face, and stomped on me. I cried and tried to run. The teacher just sat there. He pretty much let me know that I wasn't in a regular school now; things were different here.

They also let me know the rules—they were the bosses, and I had to listen to them. I didn't speak out of turn or I'd get a whopping. They weren't kidding!

If I had a problem with somebody I didn't get along with or if I didn't like somebody looking at me, I was allowed to raise my hand and tell the teacher. The teacher moved the desk out of the way, and the other kid and I would go to it.

I learned pretty quickly that I didn't need reading or writing. I trained to fight every single day, every single minute. I learned every type of move there was.

I joined a karate class, and I went every day. At that time, it was full-contact karate, not the stuff they have now. I was there for just one reason, to bust people up. I had two causes, one to get my purple belt so I could start fighting, and then to get my green belt.

I didn't get the black belt, but I beat plenty of black belts, so it didn't matter. I was there for one reason, to learn some kicks and to learn to fight, and everybody knew it. I'd fight one guy, and then I'd say, "Who's next?" Getting hit in the face didn't bother me a bit. It just fueled me to give them more. If I was ever good at something, fighting was it.

After a few years, I had such a vengefulness that I decided nobody would touch me. Nobody would mess with me! I saw people molested and raped in the bathroom at this school, but it wasn't going to happen to me. I stabbed guys with pencils, and I hit them with bowling pins.

Toward the end of my stay there, I got in a fight with a teacher. That was the end of my time at that school!

When I left there, I turned on all the vengefulness and hell that had been tied up in me for years. My brother, Jack, tried to help me by getting me a job at Ford Motors. But as soon as someone said something to me I didn't like, I knocked him out cold with a carburetor.

I got and lost a couple of other jobs before I went to work at a manufacturing company, where I met my wife. She had been going out with one of the bosses, who was about seven feet tall. Everybody was scared of this guy.

When I met somebody I thought was tough or he thought he was, I had to prove he wasn't, because, in my eyes, nine times out of ten, people were buffaloing anyway. I thought we had to get it on to see who was going to survive and who was going to win. In most cases, people don't want to go that far; I learned that fast. But I would go as far as I felt I had to go.

My future wife, Donna, and the boss broke up, and immediately I started talking with her, just to have an altercation with him, because he swore that he would bust up anybody who talked with her. We had a confrontation, but he backed down. I eventually lost that job too.

I've shot at people, and I stabbed plenty of people, but never killed anybody. I've gone to people's houses with the intention of messing them up.

There is not too much I haven't done. Somebody always wants to challenge a person with this reputation. Somebody always opened his mouth, and that is when I would beat him up.

I don't know why I got away with some of the things I did. I guess I could say I was lucky or God had a bigger plan for my life.

I swear that if Jesus hadn't come into my life at the time He did, and things hadn't changed, I would have been on the news. I had grabbed my gun plenty of times.

I can honestly say that before I started church I really didn't like anybody or anything. I used to see people hurt on the street, and I would laugh. I didn't care if they were hurt.

So one thing I know God has given me—He has given me feelings. I feel sympathy for people now. I'd never felt that before. I used to have a saying, "Do unto others before they do unto you."

When I lost my temper, I could not think; all I could see was red. I couldn't control myself. If fact, my biggest enemy, what I was most scared of, was that I always had to go through with whatever I said.

Sometimes I have a little bit of trouble, feeling as if I don't fit in and a little bit as if I'm not wanted. It is hard sometimes. I know I'm a little different; I think a little bit differently, but I'm learning, and I know I'm on a journey. I know I have a lot more on my cross to carry than some other people do, especially now that I've found out that a lot of the things I've done were wrong. I never really thought about it before; I never really cared.

I have a daughter, and it scares me sometimes to think about what I've done to other people, but I'm working on that through prayer. Pastor Hubbard has been a friend and helped me acquire knowledge. I've had brain damage because of chemicals I've used, and sometimes it's hard for me to think, but I will get through it. I'm glad I've had the chance to see how the other side lives, how to be happy and not always carrying a heavy weight, just waiting for something to happen.

I want to learn to seek God more and gain the knowledge I need to be a better person. It is hard sometimes; it's a journey and a struggle. I thank Pastor Hubbard for being my friend and talking with me and giving me wisdom. I wish somebody had done that a long time ago. I didn't have anybody to talk to before, because I didn't have any friends, and I didn't want any.

I found out one day that people at our church were scared to talk with me because they didn't know how I would react. I hope these people will not think differently of me because of what I've shared. If they knew some of the other stuff I've dealt with, some of the stuff that I've kept inside, they could understand me better. I hope they understand that I really didn't know the things I did were wrong, but I'm learning, and that's a good thing. I've been redeemed.

God bless those who've become my friends and who watch out for me and my family.

Michelle Raimondo:
Jesus Is My Second Chance

I professed being a Christian for twenty-five years, but my life did not always portray that. When I first accepted Christ as my Savior, I was on fire, full of zeal and ready to conquer the world. Instead the world conquered me.

I was saved at a Spirit-filled, Word-teaching, Bible-believing church, and I grew under the teaching of the Word. Within about five years, the pastor of the church was killed in a plane crash, my husband divorced me after twenty years of marriage, and I lost my job.

I was shaken in my Christian walk. I stopped going to church because I felt totally whipped by the devil and had no desire to go to church. I felt unworthy. After my divorce, I started living the same lifestyle I had lived before I came to know the Lord. I went to bars, partied and "enjoyed" life, or so I thought. I was raising a beautiful daughter and being led by the devil.

After about eight or nine years of that empty way of living, I began to search for a church. I went to quite a few churches but never felt like I fit in. I always felt unworthy, so I was unapproachable by the ladies. I felt as if they would never know what it was like to raise a daughter as a single, divorced woman. I thought they didn't know what it was like to work, maintain your home, raise a daughter and make it on your own. In my eyes, they had "perfect" lives.

I went to church on Sundays, after having been in the bar Saturday nights. The church I was attending didn't make me feel the least bit convicted. I searched and prayed and cried for a church where I would be brought back to the Lord.

The first time I came to United I felt the presence of the Lord and the love of God. The praise and worship brought me to the altar and dropped me to my knees. The freedom to worship as we are led is awesome.

The Word, spoken and taught at United, has pierced my heart and made it impossible for me to continue being a lukewarm Christian. The uncompromising Word of God preached here has been like a two-edged sword, slicing my heart and cutting off the flesh. I have heard the truth, and the truth is setting me free.

I have attended United Assembly of God only fourteen months, but the church's positive influence has so much changed my life in a short amount of time.

I thank God for Pastor Hubbard and his humble, obedient spirit, which keeps me in tune to the voice of God. I am so blessed to have been led here, to be accepted and to be used to reach the lost.

May God be with us and continue to bless Pastor Hubbard and anoint him to preach, teach and mentor other pastors to advance the Kingdom.

Larry Rodebach: Jesus Is My Fulfillment

Though I had been saved for many years, I only sought God when I needed Him or when I needed something from Him.

For a time, our church went through some difficulties financially and spiritually. Sometimes it got downright ugly, and our numbers dropped from about three hundred to sixty or so. It left me, a relatively new Christian, a little angry, a little frustrated and somewhat questioning what Christianity was really all about.

We had a building program, and even though we had finally moved into the lower level of the new building, most people thought it only a matter of time until the doors would close for good. However, my wife didn't think so; she kept saying, "I know there will one day be thousands here at United Assembly."

We had no pastor for a time; then Ken Hubbard, a twenty-eight-year-old youth pastor came to our church. The congregation voted him in as our senior pastor—actually, as our only pastor.

Pastor Hubbard brought us excitement, energy and a passion for souls and for Jesus Christ. The Word says that God gives us pastors as gifts, to bring us knowledge and understanding of His Word, and that is exactly what Pastor Hubbard has done in this church body and in me, personally.

As I listened to his preaching, I began to see the truths of God's Word. I heard his messages and thought about them for days. Each new understanding (at least, new to me) caused me to reach further into God.

Finally, after a couple years of his ministry, I began to seek, or ask, for the Holy Spirit to fill me. It took a little while, but one Sunday morning in February, when I wasn't really expecting it, I was filled! The "high" lasted about three days (I guess He needed to knock me upside the head).

It was a tremendous experience. I shouldn't use the word experience, because it hasn't really been that; it has been a total life change, a desire to serve God, to seek God, to know God more. I want to see people healed by God's power. I want to see every knee bow to the Creator of the universe.

I am a witness to the power of God and to His love because that love came down to me and because God gave me and United Assembly of God a gift of knowledge and understanding of His Word through Pastor Ken Hubbard.

Deborah Svrcina: Jesus Is My Peace

Coming from a single-parent home, always struggling to have just the basic needs of life met, created in me a dependence on God at a very young age, which most of my peers could not relate to.

I grew up in the church. My mother and grandmother instilled in me a deep love for the Lord and deposited in me a desire to always serve God. Even though life was very hard and sad at times, God was always there to meet those every day needs with divine surprises. Yet with all the miraculous happenings, I still never really "owned" a personal relationship with God.

Deep on the inside of me, however, I hungered for an intimate walk with the Lord on my own, to know Him personally, just for me. I have felt a call of God on my life to minister and to reach out to people since the earliest of my memories. One thing I have learned since then is that God deposits His desires into us, but the forming, perfecting and final birthing process is another story. That requires time and plenty of it (God has all the time in the world—and He uses every minute of it)!

As I approached adolescence and my young adult years, I would cry out for God to use me. But a hidden fear and a secret always haunted and taunted me, screaming louder than my heart. This horrible secret finally manifested itself full strength in my late twenties, after the birth of my second child. I had an intense self-hatred and a desire to die that almost took my life through anorexia.

My walk toward deliverance and freedom began on the

Sunday morning I first walked through the doors of Plymouth United Assembly of God. Patti Hubbard, the pastor's wife, greeted me with a friendly hello and a genuine smile. I sensed a warmth and acceptance from her that I had not felt in years.

I was truly at my lowest point, undernourished, confused and so sick that I could not even follow the order of that Sunday morning service. I wanted to get up and leave, but there was a peace present in that service that stilled my fears. I was drawn to the worship, yet I could not manage to sing even one note. I felt the presence of the Lord so strongly, with a sense of love and belonging, that I felt like I could finally rest.

However, the next few weeks gave me a close and personal look at what Job must have felt when he lost it all. I was admitted to an anorexia and bulimia treatment center in Phoenix, Arizona. For the first time in my life I was thousands of miles away from all that I called home - husband, children, family, friends and the comfort of my secret pain. Now I realized that God was all that I had. I began a six-week treatment for the initial diagnosis of an eating disorder, but there was so much more to be done on the inside—and worked outward.

How true it is. To have a deep passion for God, pain must be present at some point in this walk called life! God was answering my prayer for a personal and intimate relationship with Him; however, I didn't realize the process was going to be so painful to my flesh.

Back at home each Sunday, as I sat under Pastor Hubbard's teachings, I would leave there convinced that he was "reading my mail." No, it wasn't that; God had manna He had tailor-made for that specific body of believers to eat and be nourished by, which is precisely why He led me and my family to that church. It was a healing environment that communicated the hard truth of sin and the consequences that followed yet ministered God's awesome grace, which I could finally grasp.

Sunday after Sunday I would leave church feeling as if God had removed burdens, wrong thinking and injured emotions and replaced them with mercy, grace, love and forgiveness. What once seemed like a pointless road of life now made sense to me. Inner healing was a "course" God enrolled me in with the sole purpose of bringing about His complete and total plan for my life.

I am so blessed that He is using Plymouth United Assembly of God under the leadership and teaching of Pastor Hubbard to fulfill that plan and see it through to the end. I love this church and all of the staff members. A true sense of unity and love flows from the top and trickles down to every little sheep that is under the God-appointed leadership of our shepherd. Let the true river of healing flow. It started here for me.

Thank You, Father.

Thadd and Paula Tucker: Jesus Is Our Hope

Thadd and I came to United Assembly of God just two months after the greatest loss we've ever experienced. The baby we were in the process of adopting, and had raised as our own for the first two months of her life, was abruptly taken away from us after her birth mother changed her mind. The devastation we and our family felt was beyond words. We were in need of an emotional healing like never before.

We had a home church for many years but were in the process of making a change before this happened. We came to United with a desire to dig deeper into the Word and to continue to pray for healing.

A few months later, Pastor Hubbard had a prayer line at church for people who "needed a breakthrough before they had a breakdown." We certainly fit that description! We continued to struggle daily with the loss of our baby and desired to move forward but didn't know how.

As we walked through the prayer line, we felt the many prayers of the congregation. We also knew many friends and family from other congregations were holding us up in their prayers. In addition, we had filled out a prayer request card and knew that Pastor Hubbard was person-ally interceding for us as well.

Two months later we found out that I was pregnant! We were elated, and we continue to give God all the glory! While this great news did not take away the pain of losing a baby, it provided a distraction and hope for a happy future.

"For I know the plans I have for you," declares the
LORD, *"plans to prosper you and not to harm you,
plans to give you hope and a future."*

Jeremiah 29:11

Betty Uren: Jesus Is My Glory

In 1994, my husband and I retired to northern Michigan, on the shore of Hubbard Lake, believing that to be our permanent home. My husband, Al, did not attend church on a regular basis. In fact, in 1978, when I got on fire for God, he stopped attending altogether. And before 1978, I was a carnal Christian.

In 1998, cancer returned to Al and spread throughout his body, making it necessary for us to move back downstate for his treatments. As he became weaker, he still felt well enough to attend church, and he asked me to take him to the Methodist church where we had raised our children, so I went with him. At this time, I was attending United with my friend Dolores Arndt, and I fell in love with that ministry and the people.

Early in November 1999, an Aglow sister told me she was not satisfied with the church she and her husband were attending, so I invited her to come to United and check us out. Al knew I was meeting her that Sunday. He felt good and mentioned he would go to church with me. Needless to say, I was excited! He declined going forward, but while driving home, he mentioned returning the following week.

On November 14, 1999, when Pastor Hubbard gave the altar call, Al asked if I would walk up with him. I don't think my feet touched the floor! At the altar, Kevin Brooks ministered and prayed with him.

Al had a lot of anger and bitterness inside him, but he had such repentance that day; the tears just kept coming. He left all his anger and bitterness at the altar, and I praise

God for his salvation! Al lived only two months after that. But now I can rejoice, because I know he's in the presence of Jesus.

What a joy to know that through all the hard times, I remained faithful and kept praying and ministering to Al's needs. God's Word says that He's never early or late; He's always right on time. Praise the Lord.

I thank God for Pastor Hubbard because of his obedience to the Lord and for using the many gifts He has blessed him with. May we continue to win the lost.

I praise God for the many blessings I experience at United. Sometimes, in worship, there is such a presence of God, it's like no one else is around, only Jesus and me. I know that sounds selfish, but it's glorious!

Then there are the saints—prayer warriors like Jeri, Karen and Susie, and mentors like Larry and Pam, Phil and Colleen, and Glenda. What a privilege to work with Pastors Bob and Michelle at the Westland children's outreach. And I can't forget the loving greeting I receive every Sunday from Gib and Dean. The women at the hospitality desk—Barb, Diane, Brenda and others—are a blessing. I can't possibly mention all of them, all my friends. I am truly blessed.

Robin Wroblewski: Jesus Is My Restorer

I believe I was bitten by a tick sometime in August of 2001. I began having problems the middle of September. I had a hard time moving my hands and fingers in the morning. After a bit of flexing my fingers back and forth, I could move them almost normally, but by the middle of the day, they started to stiffen up again. Eventually they were so stiff in the morning I couldn't break an egg in my hand. Along with the stiffness came pain. The pain in my joints continued to get worse as each day went on.

After a few weeks, the stiffening started to spread to other parts of my body, moving to my elbows, ankles, knees, shoulders and jaw.

I saw a doctor in Michigan, but he was unable to determine what was wrong with me. He certainly had ideas about what was wrong, but clearly, he didn't know. He couldn't even lessen the pain, not to mention relieving the stiffness in my body.

Shortly before Thanksgiving, the pain and stiffness was so bad I could no longer work at my job as a Special Education teacher. I was no longer able to go grocery shopping, go to church or do any everyday errands.

By December the doctor was convinced that the problems were in my head, not truly real. Very few people believed me about the amount of pain I was in and my inability to move most parts of my body. Our pastor prayed for me, and he specifically prayed for a miracle in my life.

Later on that month my condition began to worsen significantly. It was so bad that my husband called me in the afternoons to make sure I could answer the phone. If I did not answer, he came home from work so the kids wouldn't come home from school and find me dead. There were times the pain was so severe that I thought I was going to die.

On January 3, 2002, I saw another doctor who thought, based on my symptoms, that I had fibromyalgia. My husband Jerry has a friend, Dennis, in Jacksonville, Florida, whom he had met only last summer, and whose sister also lives in Jacksonville with this disease. She found a neurologist there who dramatically improved her condition, so we called Dennis, got the doctor's phone number and called his office. But they said he couldn't see me for several months.

While we were on the phone, someone canceled an appointment only a few days away! God was opening the door for me to see the doctor much sooner.

The trip to Florida was very difficult for me. I was almost completely incapacitated by the time we left. My husband had to push me in a wheelchair through two airports. Sometimes I couldn't even stand up by myself. If I did, the pain did not allow me to stand for more than thirty seconds at a time. When I could walk, I could take only one step every two to four seconds. Jerry had to put his arms around my chest and pick me up. I was an invalid by the time I got to Florida.

We stayed at Jerry's dad's home, and at times, at the home of Jerry's friend, Dennis. Jerry's dad said that, when I arrived in Florida, he didn't think I was going to survive. That's how bad I looked to others.

I saw the doctor for the first time on January eighth. He was the nicest doctor I have ever dealt with, and he told us he asks God for wisdom to help each of his patients. I believe God used him to help me. He said I had an infection, which turned out to be pneumonia. He prescribed just the right medicine immediately, even though he did not yet know what else was wrong with me. Within thirty-six hours I was completely free of pain.

This was also thirty-six hours after Pastor Hubbard and the staff at United had prayed for me. After another forty-eight hours, I was able to walk and move around under my own power. I was not moving fast or for very long, but I was able to move without anyone's help for the first time in a long time.

The doctor did order me to go through some very difficult medical tests, however. Electric charges were induced into my body to test my nerves. To test my muscle response, needles were pushed into my muscles, some nearly an inch! I had a spinal tap, a nerve and muscle biopsy and a lot of blood tests. As I look back, I wonder how I made it through all that testing.

Over the next few weeks, while still in Florida, I began to get remarkably better. The doctor agreed that my recovery and the speed of my recovery were nothing short of a miracle.

At the end of January, the doctor determined I had Lyme disease, which had also caused me to be anemic. We were very shocked to hear this. Anyone who knows me knows that I am not an outdoors person at all. That a tick bit me seemed almost impossible.

The good news is that Lyme disease is completely curable, and I will have a one-hundred-percent recovery! My doctor said he had Lyme disease a few years ago. There's nothing like having a doctor who's had the same disease!

On February twelfth, I was able to return home to Michigan. I was still weak and lacked the strength and energy to do a lot of things. I got fatigued quickly, but I got stronger every day. I no longer needed the medicine I took for four months. In July I will return to Florida for another spinal tap to ensure that the disease is gone from my body.

God's hand was involved throughout this entire ordeal. Obviously, what really mattered was finding out what was wrong with me and making me better, and He did that. But there is a lot more evidence of His working in this situation.

The type of testing and the amount of testing I went through would be very difficult for any person. It was a miracle I was able to endure the testing so the doctor could get the information he needed.

God's hand was evident in my husband meeting Dennis last summer and that Dennis opened his home to us and directed us to his sister's doctor. We saw God working in enabling us to get an appointment with the doctor so quickly and in the way Jerry's dad and his wife took care of me as if I was their own daughter. Their friends in Florida checked on me often to make sure I was doing okay.

The doctor's office staff was very concerned about me. They even called after I got back home to make sure I was okay. The people at my husband's work were very understanding and gave him time off to take care of me. For several months my husband did everything around the house.

I am so thankful to the Lord for sparing my life. I now appreciate all of the little things that I used to take for granted. God heard every prayer and answered them for me. I continue to see restoration in my body. People everywhere say that I am a miracle, and it is a witness to them. This is my testimony: God spared my life! I will never forget how He touched me.

Conclusion: Jesus Is Love in Action

On February 4, 2003, a home cell group from United Assembly of God was meeting in the home of Bill and Ellen Pye. In the midst of praise and worship, the phone rang. Ellen Pye answered the phone. The caller asked for Bob Wolf, one of the members of the group, so Bob took the call.

On the other end of the line was a man named David Spencer, who was not known by Bob. David explained to Bob that his car had broken down as he was passing through the area on his way to Flint to begin a new job. He was calling from the lobby of the Red Roof Inn along the interstate. He had no money to pay for a room and asked Bob if he would put him up for the night. He said it was too cold to sleep in the car, but that if Bob could help him with accommodations, he would work on the car in the morning and then be gone, with no further need to bother him.

As Bob spoke with David on the Pyes' phone, his own cell phone rang. It was his wife, Jo, so he put David on hold while he talked with her. She had not gone to the cell group meeting that night because she had not been feeling well. She explained that David had called their home looking for Bob; he believed Bob to be the pastor of United. He had given Jo the same story he had just explained to Bob. Jo had felt that something needed to be done for this man, but was unsure about whether or not she should interrupt the cell group meeting. While considering what to do, she had felt something inside of her say, "Okay, you know how to pray, but do you know how to obey?" Sensing she was to go ahead and help, she had given David the Pyes' home number, telling him to contact Bob there.

After hearing Jo's story, Bob returned to David's call and asked why David had contacted him specifically. David explained that he had called the Plymouth Township Police and told them about his being stranded; he had asked if there were any churches in the area that might help him. Immediately, they had thought of United and gave David the name and number of the first person listed on that church's emergency contact list.

As soon as the cell group meeting was over, the cell group gathered around Bob and two others who would go with him to pray for their safety. The three men left to meet David Spencer.

David turned out to be a big, two-hundred forty pound fellow of imposing stature. The men took care of checking him into the hotel and paid for his room.

Before leaving, Bob felt impressed to question David about his spiritual condition. He told Bob that he was not serving the Lord at the present time. Bob asked if he would like to get his life right with God right then. David, however, was not ready. He explained to Bob that in a former church he had once been very active and on fire for the Lord; however, he had suffered a huge disappointment, which had soured him on the church and religion in general. He was still carrying the bitterness of his experience, was living in a backslidden condition, and was not ready to recommit his life to the Lord. The men from United promised to uphold David in prayer They exchanged addresses with him, and then the four men went their separate ways.

Here is a testimony in the making. Whether it is Bob's story, David's story, or the story of one of the others involved, the Lord Jesus Christ was at work in this situation. Bob and the other men obediently walked out the actions that Love Himself would have done in order to help someone who was in trouble.

This testimony could have been yours. It could have been your neighbor's, or your brother's, or your son's or daughter's. While we may not know what has become of David today, we do know that he experienced God that night in the form of a seed of love sown by the men in the cell group. What if Bob had decided that David's call was too suspicious and had told him he was on his own? What if Jo had not followed the leading of the Spirit and had not given David the phone number where Bob could be reached? What if the township police had never heard of United Assembly because we had never built a reputation as a caring church?

God calls us to be a caring people. Whenever opportunities arise that test our faith, we must be ready to seize those moments by responding positively with a cheerful heart.

Love is an action, and we are to love others so that the world can see and know who Jesus Christ is.

United has grown from a small, struggling church that averaged eighty-eight people on Sunday mornings to a strong, vibrant church with nearly one hundred ministries. The church that the devil tried to close down, God has chosen to prosper and bless! He *is* building His church!

Who do *you* say that He is?